J. ALLAN CASH
Camera Globetrotter

J. ALLAN CASH
Camera Globetrotter

J. ALLAN CASH F.I.I.P., F.R.P.S.

FOUNTAIN PRESS

13–35 Bridge Street, Hemel Hempstead, Hertfordshire, England.

Model and Allied Publications Limited,
Fountain Press,
Book Division, Station Road, Kings Langley,
Hertfordshire, England

First Published 1973
© J. Allan Cash, 1973
ISBN 0 85242 333 ʊ

Bookjacket printed by
Alpine Press, Watford, Hertfordshire, England

Colour origination by
Sun Litho, Ruislip, Middlesex, England

Colour printing by
The Saffron Press, Saffron Walden, Essex, England

Text composition in 11 pt Photon Times
Text Printing and binding by
The Pitman Press, Bath, Somerset, England

Contents

	PHOTOGRAPHER'S WIFE by Betty Cash	vii
One	MY EARLY DAYS	1
Two	THE SOVIET UNION	9
Three	THE BALKANS	15
Four	THE YEAR OF THE WAR	26
Five	IN THE ARMY	30
Six	THE BRITISH COUNCIL	40
Seven	FREELANCING AGAIN	44
Eight	COMMISSIONED TRIPS	55
Nine	AROUND AFRICA	60
Ten	SOUTH AFRICA AND RHODESIA	66
Eleven	THE FAR EAST	82
Twelve	MORE COMMISSIONED TRIPS	95
Thirteen	CHINA	104
Fourteen	NORTH AMERICA	109
Fifteen	AUSTRALIA AND AROUND THE WORLD	114
Sixteen	INDIA AND THE FAR EAST AGAIN	118
Seventeen	BOTH SIDES OF THE RED SEA	123
Eighteen	CONCLUSION	126
Appendix	THE BUSINESS SIDE	129

List of Illustrations

1 Bulgarian Harvest (Photo by Betty Cash) 2 The Moscow Circus
3 Dar es Salaam, Tanzania 4 Amboseli, Kenya
5 Gnu, Amboseli Game Reserve, Kenya 6 Lion in Lake Manyara
National Park, Tanzania 7 Chicago, USA
8 Las Vegas, Nevada, USA 9 Grand Canyon, Arizona, USA
10 A boy of the Ndebele tribe, South Africa
11 A peasant in Nepal 12 A miner off duty in South Africa
13 A wandering minstrel in Nepal (Photo by Betty Cash)
14 Indian woman carrying water near Delhi
15 Temple at Kelaniya, Ceylon 16 Pilgrims on the Ghats
at Benares, India 17 Buddha at Kamakura, Japan
18 Television studio at Riyadh, Saudi Arabia 19 Mount Fuji
from Izu Peninsula, Japan 20 Ghost gum in the Outback,
Australia 21 Milford Sound, in the Fiordland National Park,
New Zealand 22 Great Wall of China in the mountains
north of Peking 23 Steel workers at the Wuhan Steel Works,
China
24 Demonstrators dispersing, Peking

Photographer's Wife

BY BETTY CASH

There are so many fishing, tennis and golf widows in this world; I did not wish to become a darkroom widow! That, I think, was when my interest in photography began. I realised long ago, when I met Allan on a ship in the Baltic, and when we wandered round Leningrad and Moscow together, that one could soon become bored or impatient waiting for one's photographic companion while he studied the sky or the sun which was reluctant to appear. So why not do the same and have fun competing? I had been interested in travel long before I met Allan, and could see how the two went beautifully together.

I started off with a Leica, but never felt happy with it or my photographic results. It was only when I had my first Rolleiflex that I became really enthusiastic about photography. Allan was kindness itself during my first efforts and it was his encouragement and advice that helped me to enjoy taking pictures and to become a professional. Indeed he has trained me so well to his methods, that often I have unknowingly taken a photograph from the exact spot he has chosen. He always told me I could write and here again, gave me a lot of guidance.

One of the first things I was taught was never to take an outdoor scenic picture without sunlight. In the early days, it seemed such a pity not to record a glorious part of the world with my camera, just because the skies were grey, but how right Allan was. When one returns and looks at the sparkle and brilliance of a photograph taken in the right conditions, then the others, which I call forced pictures, are ready for the scrap heap. I have since learned to be patient and careful or do without. Consequently few of my photographs are scrapped. I now work exclusively with a Rolleiflex and use Kodak Tri-X or Ektachrome film. At one time, I took only monochrome photographs, now I do colour nearly all the time. When I travel alone I use two Rolleiflex cameras, for monochrome and colour.

We are both gregarious and love meeting people, and our work affords us the opportunity of doing this. I have been a member of the Women's Press Club for many years (now amalgamated with the Fleet Street Press Club) and we are both members of the Guild of Travel Writers. At the various meetings and functions organised by these Clubs, we have met many famous and interesting personalities. I well remember being introduced to the Queen Mother who had honoured the Women's Press Club with a visit. Allan and I were leaving in a few days for a long tour of the Far East and this was mentioned to her. She was most interested and we talked about Hong Kong. When she was saying goodbye to us all, she turned to me and said she hoped I would have an enjoyable trip. She was modest and charming.

Meeting Archbishop Makarios was exciting. We were granted an interview with him in his Palace in Nicosia, yet when we arrived, we found a large group of press people. We thought we had had it, and waited with the others until it was time to go. As we were leaving, one of his aides came over to us and said:

'Mr. and Mrs. Cash, Archbishop Makarios is ready to see you now.' It was a delightfully informal interview. He wanted to know what we had seen in Cyprus and we agreed that the Troodos Mountains are one of the highlights of that beautiful island. He readily posed for us in his office and then in the garden, and later he returned one of our photographs of him duly autographed.

A lady who has always charmed us is Dame Flora McLeod of McLeod. We have had tea with her in Dunvegan Castle several times, and recently we found it hard to believe that she was in her nineties. She is young in mind and figure, and on this last occasion was telling us of her plans to revisit Australia. One is always assured of a warm welcome from Dame Flora at Dunvegan Castle.

When we are on an assignment on board ship, I keep a sharp lookout for photogenic types, not only glamourous girls in bikinis, but older people who might fit in with the kind of pictures often wanted. These contacts have led to some excellent studies of life on board, and some of the models have become our good friends over the years.

People often say to us:

'What a wonderful life you two have'. Of course it is thrilling to visit new countries, to see new people and their way of life, but a tremendous amount of work and organization goes with it before and after a trip. I do not think I have ever said to Allan: 'I haven't the right clothes for this trip', or 'What shall I wear?' for a particular function. He always seems to be happy with my choice and often tells me so. He hates going into shops and I have never asked him to accompany me on one of my shopping expeditions.

When we plan our journeys for the year, I make a mental note of the type of country to be visited, the climate, time of year, etc., inspect my existing wardrobe and purchase one or two additional items well in advance. Mostly, I wear good well cut classic clothes, buying accessories to bring myself up to high fashion. On a round-the-world trip, I used interchangeables and man-made fibres which travel well, and only one of everything needed for the entire trip which lasted three and a half months. This included going on safari in the outback of Australia, a cruise round the islands of Fiji, Christmas in Hawaii, and staying with friends in the Diplomatic Corps in San Francisco for a week over the New Year. This required some careful planning but presented no problems.

When we are travelling together and Allan has an industrial assignment lined up, I go off on my own with my cameras. I like nothing better that to have time to stand and stare and, if weather conditions are good, I feel elated and forget time.

While manoeuvring for a 'contre jour' shot in Singapore a short while ago, I was confronted by a tourist laden with cameras.

'Lady' he said, 'you'll never get a picture shooting like that. Always have the sun behind you'.

When I replied that my editor wanted it that way, he walked sheepishly away.

People sometimes ask me what part I play in our organization. What do I do myself? After explaining that I really do take many of the photographs, I sometimes add:

'I write the nonsense. My husband writes the serious stuff.'

I once said this in a radio interview in Capetown. The following morning I received a telegram from the *Johannesburg Star* asking me to do three articles for them on nonsense. I had to sit down there and then and think what I really meant by nonsense!

I am invariably asked which is my favourite country and it is always difficult to reply. There are so many places I long to revisit in Europe and the Far East, each with its particular charm, beauty and people. The thought of New York had always scared me. Yet when we were there for the first time, I was fascinated. It is surely ready-made for the photographer, with endless sky-scraper angles, it's downtown brashness, and its fine wide avenues. I was the complete tourist, enthralled with the view from the Empire State Building, the Lincoln Centre, and just walking round the Rockefeller courtyard with its fine display of flowers. The shops are a paradise for women and I spent far too long window gazing.

I hope we shall have an opportunity of returning to New Orleans, a part of America that is still very French, the original town of Dixeyland. How different was the sound of jazz in those old halls. Of course, we ate superb French food at Antoines, walked endlessly in the old French quarter, and admired the many magnificent houses with their swimming pools.

Another country that I find exciting is Israel. I want to stay once more on a kibbutz, to look down on the harbour of Haifa at sunset with the thousands of lights twinkling like little stars, and to walk by the Sea of Galilee. A great country and a great people.

For many years I always declared that Kashmir was the most beautiful area on earth. Then I visited Nepal, alone the first time, and now I think this dramatic little mountain kingdom has become my favourite.

Best of all, I love coming home. On the way from London Airport, we always seem to say how green and clean it is, and when we walk into our lovely garden on the edge of Hampstead Heath, I know that I would not wish to live anywhere else in the world. It is marvellous to get into my kitchen and try out a new recipe I have collected in some part of the world, to listen to our record collection and later to see the result of our photographic work. Yet after a while, I am just as keen as ever for new adventures.

CHAPTER ONE

My Early Days

A resumé of my first book

I was born in the early years of the century in a tiny village in the heart of Cheshire. Later, a brother and a sister appeared on the scene and we were a happy middle-class family. My father worked in Manchester, in insurance and he did well, in the days before the First World War, when life was orderly and predictable, when security and stability were highly prized. His ideas for me later on ran to a steady job with good prospects in some respectable firm, where I could make progress year by year and end up with a pension. My ideas were somewhat different.

I believed that life was a glorious adventure, full of interest and excitement, if only one could find the key to it. I hated the thought of monotony and routine, doing the same thing day after day. And I was afflicted with an insatiable wanderlust, a powerful desire to travel and see the world. This hit me quite early in my teens, though I could not for the life of me see how it was going to be done. Package holidays and student tours at cheap prices were unheard of in those days. Travel was for the rich, it seemed, and always would be, and I was a long way from being rich.

I was at school all through the First World War and at the end of it my all-absorbing hobby was radio. Those were early days, well before broadcasting was even thought of. Everything was done in morse code, and before I could obtain a transmitting license, I had to pass a test in morse signalling. We amateurs were restricted to certain unwanted wave-lengths where we would not interfere with commercial stations. I made radio friends all over Europe, then further afield, and my signals were even picked up in New Zealand, all from a tiny set of home-made equipment that was hardly powerful enough to light a small lamp. The work that amateurs did all over the world proved to commercial radio companies the great potentialities of short waves and low power and must have been responsible for much re-thinking in technical circles.

During those early radio days I tried my hand at writing articles for radio magazines on the equipment I made myself and on my experiences in general. Some of them were published, so I must have had the spark of journalism hidden somewhere in my being. Curiously enough, I did not do any photography then,

When I needed pictures to illustrate my articles, I got a friend to do them for me. I had only dabbled in photography as a boy, with a box camera, developing my own films and making daylight prints for my family and friends.

My first employment after leaving school was, naturally, in radio. I found during my first few years that I could get work, making and repairing radio sets after broadcasting came in, and so on, but it never seemed to lead anywhere. I was not making real progress. So I cut my ties with Britain and went to Canada. A half-cousin of mine, John Barnaby, also a radio 'ham', had gone there a couple of years earlier, and he had done well. He had started work unloading railway trucks but soon got a job with a big radio firm and was now well established. I wrote and asked him what chances I would have.

'If you are expecting to find a soft job in your own line right away,' he replied, 'don't come! If you are prepared to work at anything, from navvying upwards, until you find your feet, then there's plenty of opportunity in Canada.'

Going to Canada was quite a step for me. I had never been out of the country before, I had very little money—certainly not enough to get back home if I failed—I hated leaving my family circle and I frankly admit that I had more than one moment of panic once my decision was made. Today, young people do far more than ever I did in the way of early travelling, without batting an eyelid, but it was not quite the same in those days. It was a great relief to know that John would meet me in Montreal and that I could stay with him to start with.

I made all the arrangements before telling my parents. They thought I had gone crazy, but were generous enough to pay my fare. I sailed on a cargo ship from Manchester and once clear of Liverpool, with the land sinking astern, I began to feel that I was launching out on a great adventure. And I have never lost the spirit of adventure from that day to this. Even today I get excited at the prospect of a new trip looming up, wherever it may take me.

Canada was a success. I found a job within a few days in a radio shop, making and repairing radio sets, at $20 per week. I got a rise in three weeks, I became manager in seven and I left in ten weeks because I felt that an average working day of twelve hours, six days a week, was too much of a good thing. I was taken on by the Northern Electric Company, where I worked happily for some nine years. First I helped to run their own radio station. Those were early days, when we made much of the equipment with our own hands, and did a lot of experimenting. Then I did a lot of public address work, installing loud speakers and microphones when this was very much of a novelty, which is hard to believe today. Then came talking pictures, in 1928, and I was promoted to installation engineer, putting in the new equipment in theatres all over the western half of Canada, from Winnipeg to the Pacific coast.

One reason I was so happy in Canada was the amount of travelling I was able to do. Even before talking pictures came along, I had trips up to northern Ontario mining towns, to Quebec and Toronto, installing and operating equipment. I even had to go to Banff, in the Rockies, a three day train journey each way. Some of the equipment was missing when I arrived, and so I had a week to go climbing mountains and exploring while it was being replaced. I liked the west so much that, during a holiday, I got myself a job on the Canadian National Railway, guarding Chinese transients all the way from Montreal to Vancouver, and then went off with a game warden friend for a couple of weeks on horse-back in the Rockies. I bought a huge motor cycle and had two holidays on it, one down through the New England states of America from Montreal, the other down the Pacific coast from Vancouver.

On all these trips I took a folding camera with me and tried to illustrate my experiences. Later on, I sometimes wrote articles on business trips for the company magazine. But still I was not taking photography seriously. Then came the depression of the early 1930's, and that jolted me into action. I was lucky not to lose my job, but in fact I was given a new one, as service engineer at Belleville, Ontario, looking after a dozen cinemas scattered over a wide range of country. I had to make regular visits and also be on call for emergencies. This gave me a lot of spare time where I could do what I liked as long as I was on call after 2 p.m. each working day.

I took up writing and photography, intent on having a second string to my fiddle in case of the worst. I studied books and photographic magazines, I bought an Auto-Graflex Jnr. camera, and I started to take pictures seriously. I had no one to teach me, so I learnt the hard way, by trial and error. I bought an enlarger, blacked out a room where I was living, and taught myself to print and develop. It was not easy and I was very slow. But it came in the end.

Soon I began to send out pictures to editors, after studying their magazines and newspapers. I never tried news photography; it has never really interested me. I like to work more leisurely. I had a few successes and was thus spurred on to try even harder. I took a picture of live cattle being loaded on to a ship in Montreal, wrote a short article and it was published in the *Manchester Evening News.* I sent pictures quite often to the *Manchester Guardian,* as Readers' Photographs, of which they published a lot. I had quite a few successes here, at half a guinea a time, but the money was not important to me then.

Subjects for single pictures that were successful included a bear up a tree from quite a close range, which I sold several times. Winter subjects in Quebec and Ontario, showing much snow and ice, more than are normally seen in Britain, went down well. Also typical Canadian scenery. The Ottawa Peace Tower, floodlit, just before the Ottawa Conference of the 1930's, sold only once, to my great disappointment. It seemed to me to be a natural but I was wrong. I did a lot of nature photography, especially wild flowers in situ, and such birds and animals as I could get at, as well as pets—dogs and kittens.

I had some pictures published by the Toronto Star Weekly, and indeed this remained a steady market for me for many years, long after I left Canada. I wrote articles for certain photographic magazines in the U.S.A. and in England, and a few were published. I became almost a regular contributor to a farming magazine in Canada, with articles and pictures on nature subjects and later a whole series on photography for the amateur. I was always looking at magazines and guessing what I could send to them. These successes sound wonderful but it is hard to convey any idea of the amount of work they entailed, and the frequent disappointments which occurred all the time. One has to be an optimist in this game and not take reverses too seriously.

In 1933 I decided to be reckless and go on a short cruise to Bermuda, from Montreal. It was a great success. Firstly, I took many photographs on board ship, of ports of call, and as much of Bermuda as I could manage in a short time. Secondly, this trip showed me that there was a great big interesting world just over my little horizon, and I vowed that somehow I was going to see more of it. Thirdly, there was a man on the ship who changed my life. He was, eventually, the spur I needed to get me out of my all too comfortable rut into the outside world. He was known to one and all as Jay, and he had made a big name for himself with the new candid photography in a weekly Toronto magazine known as *Saturday Night*. He saw me at work and we got talking. He only travelled from Montreal to Quebec but that was enough.

I met Jay often later in Toronto. He showed me how he worked and before long he converted me to 35 mm photography. He had made his name on the Leica. I bought one and an enlarger and found that I could adapt myself to the small negatives quite easily. Jay was a stickler for fine grain and his insistence on avoiding grainy pictures was the most excellent training for me. So much so that, when I see grain used today deliberately as an effect, it almost makes me writhe. We always reckoned that any negative that could not produce a 20 × 16 inch enlargement without the grain being obvious was not worth keeping. Colour photography was hardly known, comparatively, in those days. There was little market for it and so I did no colour work. How different today!

I worked harder than ever back at Belleville. I had always been interested in natural history. My father was an authority on British birds, while my mother knew all the wild flowers. Living in the country all my early life, I grew up in this atmosphere of loving the countryside and knowing a good deal about it. Belleville was a small country town in an area of rich farmland. Fifty miles to the north the wilderness began, a vast land of lakes and hills and forests which stretched right up to the Arctic, virtually unbroken and much of it unknown.

I explored locally far and wide and did a lot of nature photography. I took pictures of many wild flowers, as they grew in the woods and fields, and these made good subjects for articles both in America and in Britain. I particularly studied wild orchids in Canada. Surprisingly, there are more than a hundred different kinds, some of them most spectacular and colourful. I met an old man who was one of the recognized authorities on the wild orchids of North America, and once he was satisfied that I was a genuine flower lover, he took me out to various remote spots, some hidden amidst farmland, others in the wilderness of the north, and we had some wonderful days together. He showed me one lady slipper so rare that he doubted if more than fifty people had ever knowingly seen it. Yet it was within two miles of another small town.

I bought a close-focusing device for the Leica, with extension tubes, and could thus photograph flowers close up. I always put the camera on an old extendable tripod, one which I did not mind digging down into soft earth or mud to make the camera steady. In order to get enough depth of field, I often had to close the aperture down to a small opening. This meant longer exposures than normal, sometimes in the order of half a second or more. Hence the tripod. I always exposed by means of a cable release. The main trouble with flowers is wind movement and this called for a lot of patience. I found that a hazy day, bright but without strong sunlight, was best for flowers, as no hard shadows were then produced among the petals.

I explored various woods and swamps doing this flower photography. In Canada there are many sphagnum swamps, often heavily covered with cedar trees growing in the water. They are dangerous places because they often contain hidden holes of water and mud, camouflaged by greenery growing on the surface. Also, it is remarkably easy to get lost in such swamps. I always either used a compass or took a careful bearing on the sun and figured out where it should be when I came out, so that I would start for home in the right direction and not get myself hopelessly, and perhaps dangerously, lost. It was all good fun and I found many beautiful flowers. I was sometimes bitten by mosquitoes so much that by the end of the season I became almost immune to their stings.

Another form of nature photography that I did, actually before my Leica days, was to take pictures of a family of tree swallows at a nest box on the side of my house. I used a folding camera with a proxar lens, and I fixed this up on a wooden bracket two and a half feet from the nest box. I sat on a nearby balcony and released the shutter by means of a piece of string. Each time I pulled it I had to go up a step ladder and wind on the film. The birds became so used to me that they often went into the nest box while I was on the ladder, and I even took a few pictures like that, with my head within two feet of the birds. It was a delightful job and I sold these pictures many times later on.

In 1934 I came back to England for the first time, taking a few weeks' unpaid leave and adding it to my holidays. There were no air services in those days, so nearly three weeks of my holiday was spent on the Atlantic. My parents gave me a wonderful welcome and took me all round some of the loveliest parts of the south of England before going to their home in Cheshire. Then I had a week in London, during which I went to see several editors. This was most valuable, as I was able to put various suggestions to them for articles and photographs, and not only did I get an immediate answer but I learnt more exactly what they wanted. I met Percy Harris who was then editor of a magazine called *Modern Photography,* and who had published one or two of my articles. He, too, had started life in radio and later transferred to photography. Many years later he became President of the Royal Photographic Society. He remained a good friend of mine until his death.

Later in my holiday, we all went up to Scotland for two weeks in my family's car. This was a great joy to me, as I had not been to Scotland before. I noticed many things about roads, traffic and safety measures in Britain and could not help comparing them with Canada. Later on, I sent an article to the *Daily Telegraph,* comparing road conditions and traffic in the two countries. I was even bold enough to suggest a few ways in which Britain might copy Canada. To my delight, this was published on the editorial page, my first real feature article in any prominent paper.

My trip produced a large number of new pictures which I proceeded to exploit as widely as I could, in Canada, U.S.A. and of course back in England, too. Now my appetite for travelling was truly whetted and I knew something must happen soon. The following year I went on a long trip, as my holiday, with Jay, all down through the Maritime Provinces of Canada, i.e. Nova Scotia, New Brunswick and Prince Edward Island, as well as eastern Quebec. This again produced many new pictures. But the most important thing was that I was able to discuss with Jay my future and whether I should quit my radio job and start out in photography.

I did not think I had really got far enough, but he had too much work to do, including much industrial photography, and finally we decided that I should join him on a trial basis in Toronto. He certainly did not promise me anything dramatic but we both thought we could work together and expand his existing business, together with mine, until it could really support both of us properly. On the way back through Montreal I called in to see my supervisor at the Northern Electric Company. I knew him well and I told him what the situation was and asked him for his advice. He said, without hesitation:

'If I had your chance, I'd take it like a shot. There are no prospects for any of us here for years to come.'

That decided me and not long afterwards I left the Northern, my nice comfortable job at Belleville, where no one ever came to bother me from the Company, where I had lots of spare time and where I had become integrated into the very pleasant life of a small country town in Canada. It was a big gamble, but once made, there was no going back. My father was quite horrified and thought I must have gone totally mad.

Working with Jay was a most valuable experience, in many different ways. We did a lot of industrial photography, dramatizing sometimes mundane processes, and I realized how useful the Leica camera could be for this sort of work, where lighting was dim and where human expressions were often an important ingredient of the picture. I became quite fascinated with this sort of candid industrial photography and later on made this one of my main lines, developing my own technique. I had a number of picture features in *Saturday Night,* Jay insisting on my name appearing whenever the pictures were mine.

We worked together all through one winter, but in the end things did not work out right. We never quarrelled but our methods of business were so fundamentally different that I began to see that I should have to do something else. A sad state of affairs, as I had burnt my boats now and could not go back to my radio work. I never even thought of it. I had started something new and this I must follow. Jay became involved in books which looked as though they would become his main interest, and this was something we could not do together. What should I do?

'Go travelling, Allan,' Jay advised. 'You know how to take photographs and you can write. The whole wide world is before you. Find a way to travel cheaply and there is no limit to what you can do.'

I received a lot of encouragement from Willson Woodside, a lecturer at Toronto University, who went off every summer holiday across to Europe where he travelled widely, and very cheaply, then wrote political and economic articles, many for *Saturday Night*. Later he became editor of this paper but that was long after I had left Canada. He had mastered the art of crossing the Atlantic for a dollar per day, on cargo ships, something that could be done in those days if you had time and got on the right side of the captain. I decided to try and do the same thing.

I went down to New York, by bus in order to save money. I put up at a cheap hotel and did a round of shipping offices, without any luck at all. Montreal port was closed by ice during the winter, so I could not try there. No one would offer me a trip on their ships. Why should they? I was a total stranger to them and I really had nothing to offer in return, a lesson that came in useful in later years. As a final resort I used an introduction someone had given me to Intourist, the Soviet travel organization.

I was genuinely interested in the great socialist experiment going on in Russia, a bit starry-eyed perhaps, but this rubbed off and the manager took my suggestion of going to Russia seriously. He said he could arrange a trip at a much reduced rate, if I could promise that *Saturday Night* would publish at least two articles on my impressions. He laid down no stipulation that my articles must be favourably slanted; he just took a chance. We pored over maps and made an ambitious itinerary. He told me what it would cost me and I decided that my savings would stand the strain. But he could not get me there. I must get to Leningrad by my own efforts. And that posed a problem.

I went back to Toronto. Jay was enthusiastic, but more important, the editor of *Saturday Night*, Mr. Sandwith, whom I had got to know quite well, said:

'You bet I'll take two articles, at least, on your observations in Russia.'

I was as good as there, I felt. That seems to me to be the journalistic mind. You never work out every detail and weigh everything up, as a sensible business-trained person would do. You see your ultimate objective clearly and you just go to it. The details will somehow sort themselves out. All I had to do was get from Toronto to Leningrad, on very little money!

I went round to see the manager of the Canadian Pacific Steamship Company and told him my problem. We worked out what it would cost, travelling third class everywhere. I told him I could not possibly afford it. Then he said:

'Alright, let's see what we can do. I would like you to travel by our line, as you may mention it in articles later.'

That was more like it. I finished up with a first class railway ticket from Toronto to St. John, New Brunswick, a first class cabin on one of their passenger ships from there to Liverpool, a railway ticket from Liverpool to London and a second class passage on a Soviet ship from London to Leningrad, all for the price of a third class ticket across the Atlantic. I was in the travel business!

Woodside was enthusiastic about my plans. He had been to Russia but was not very much impressed with it. But he said it did not matter where I went. I was making a start and he just knew I would be a success. He gave me some good advice, to settle those fears that inevitably arise—what happens if I get myself stranded somewhere?

'Don't worry,' he said, 'no matter how lost you get, how little of any language you can speak, you will never starve. You will find people of every nation helpful and friendly. It's a glorious adventure you are going on. Treat it as such and make the most of it.'

I am sure young people today go off on far more adventurous trips than I was doing, without a worry in their heads. But I was launching out to make a success of photo-journalism and literally everything depended on this trip being a success. It was costing me my total savings. If it did not pay, and soon, I had a problem.

CHAPTER TWO

The Soviet Union

When I arrived in England my family, glad though they were to see me, thought I was completely crazy to have thrown up everything in Canada. But I stayed with them at home until my visa arrived. Then I went to London and boarded the SIBIR, one of the smart Soviet ships which sailed literally from London Bridge. There were eighty-five passengers on board, an interesting and very mixed crowd.

It took five days to reach Leningrad, via the Kiel Canal. During those five days an English doctor and a nurse, passengers on board, became very friendly and eventually married, in England. I became very friendly with a bright and sparkling girl called Betty, whose parents were Russian, living in London. Later on we also were married and Betty has helped me greatly to build up my business, becoming an excellent photographer herself. We four have been the best of friends ever since and visit each other frequently. There's a lot to be said for travelling by sea!

I was to spend two months in the Soviet Union. My itinerary included a number of cities and different regions, starting in Leningrad and going through Moscow, then Kharkov, Rostov on Don, and the Caucasus, round the Black Sea coast to Yalta, and finally to Odessa and Kiev. During those weeks I took hundreds of pictures of just about everything I could, in town and country, on sea and land. I began to build up a series of photographs on various themes and to get ideas for articles. I got into trouble only once, in Moscow, when the police took a film out of my camera. I had photographed some forbidden building without knowing it. They were firm but quite polite.

All films exposed in the Soviet Union pre-war had to be developed in the country and shown to the police on leaving. I therefore had to develop every film I took while I was there. It was quite impractical to have them done by the Russians. So I carried a Correx tank, lots of packets of developer, a tin of fixer, two bottles, a thermometer, a sponge for wiping down the films, and a lot of film clips. Every night I developed films in my room, often until quite late. It was summer time and quite warm, so they were always dry by the morning. I rolled them up and kept them in the little tins they originally came in, to keep them clean and free of dust, all numbered to tally with my note-book. It was quite a job. Sometimes the cold water out of the taps was as high as 80°F., so cooling my solutions was difficult. I had to develop at a wide range of temperatures, but somehow it worked.

On the SIBIR I learnt much about the Soviet Union. There were various

Russians returning home after studying their particular subjects abroad and they gave us lectures, telling us of their new lives.

I became friendly with Guy Philips, a young journalist who had lived in Russia for a year and was now returning to see what changes were taking place. He spoke Russian fluently and was most useful to me. I took many pictures on board, and saw how the Russians ran their ship. We went through the Kiel Canal and I took a number of pictures in the locks, until I was stopped by the German police on shore. When the war started a few years later I gave the War Office a set of these pictures, but I never heard if they were of any use to anyone.

Visitors to Russia paid for everything before going to the country, and were given coupons in return to cover meals, hotels, transport and one sight-seeing trip each day. I went on all these trips and found them most useful, though often too short. I went around a lot on my own, poking into side streets, walking everywhere, even going by tram and the Moscow Underground, and walking miles in the country wherever I could. Guy and I also went round a lot together. One day we took a train from Moscow with a friend of his and had a marvellous day in the country, at a sort of holiday camp.

I had a few days in Leningrad first, finding this a beautiful city on the banks of the Neva, with wide streets and of course wonderful palaces and churches. But, oh, how badly everything needed a coat of paint. Most of the churches were closed or converted into museums, but the palaces and art galleries were in full use and most popular, with crowds of peasants and workers almost worshipping the paintings, world masterpieces by virtually all the famous painters. The Hermitage is, of course, the most renowned and indeed it may well contain more art treasures than any similar building in the world. The Soviets have certainly looked after their art inheritance in a commendable way.

In Moscow the Metro was being built, amidst great enthusiasm. People in every kind of job worked in a voluntary capacity on their days off, eager to do their bit, emerging from underground plastered with mud and swaggering off home with great pride. And certainly the Metro was a great success. A few lines were already open. Not only did they relieve the traffic problem above ground, but the whole thing was a work of art. The trains were wide and clean and looked as if they were polished every day. The stations were each designed by a different architect and were more like palaces, decorated with all manner of marble, stained glass, statuary and the most elaborate lighting. It was exciting to travel on the Metro, and quite easy.

The Moscow River in those days was normally reduced to a muddy trickle during the summer months. But a great scheme was under way of raising the banks and building boulevardes and wide highways along both sides. I took pictures of both men and women doing this work. Later, the level of the water was raised by many feet and on subsequent visits I saw how effective the whole project had been. Moscow's river is now widely used, with some handsome pleasure boats, and is a great asset to the city all the way along.

I took every opportunity to visit collective farms in different parts of the country, and made up a big set of pictures on them. Many of the collectives were excellent, a far cry from the former days of miserable poor peasants being ruthlessly exploited. I saw farming being done by modern methods, with machinery; there were club rooms and creches, laboratories and new houses, though this development was by no means even. I saw some far less prosperous collectives from trains on which I travelled. Despite all this collective work, the farm workers still valued the little plots of land round their own homes, and tended to spend too much time on them, for they could sell the products from them on the open market. Human nature does not change instantly with political systems.

I liked Moscow on that first visit and I have liked it ever since. Despite its enormous recent growth, it is still one of the cities of the world that I really like to wander about in, to explore on foot. The Red Square is magnificent and unique, and now one can wander all through the Kremlin, with its famous palaces and glorious churches. I could not do that in 1936. But I did go through Lenin's tomb, where his body is preserved—a highly complicated and very clever piece of work—and I did not have to queue up with thousands of Russians patiently waiting to do the same thing. Being a foreign visitor I was allowed to go right in, but my camera was taken from me and returned as I came out.

The most exciting thing I did, perhaps, in the Soviet Union was to go by road, in a small open bus, from Ordjonikidze, in the North Caucasus, over the Georgian Military Highway to Tiflis, the capital of Georgia. This is a famous road, built many years ago right through the Caucasus Mountains, through deep gorges, over high passes and past many fortified villages. The scenery was dramatic and the hill tribesmen most exotic and often colourful, in sheep-skin hats and long flowing cloaks, many riding on horseback. I was delighted when we got a flat tyre and I was able to get out and take pictures, in one of the most spectacular parts of the road.

Tiflis, or Tbilisi as it is now known, was, and still is a most beautiful city, especially its main street which is lined with many great cedar trees. The steep little cobbled streets in the old part of the town, full of strange people, donkeys and overhanging eaves, are now, alas, no more. They have all been wiped out and replaced by more modern buildings and wider streets, but it has all been done very well and in keeping.

I went on to Erivan, the capital of Armenia, by train. Here was a strange mixture of mud huts and modern blocks of flats, all side by side, but it was an attractive town. From its streets I looked up to the summit of Mount Ararat and was to see this many years later from Turkey, to the south. I flew back to Tiflis, for a very small extra sum. I was the only passenger that day and I flew in a little two-seater plane in an open cockpit, complete with flying jacket and helmet. Alas, I was not allowed to take pictures, a pity, because we flew low over mountain passes and close to great peaks gleaming with glaciers in the bright sunlight.

I spent three days on a modern passenger ship sailing from Batum round the Black Sea coast to Yalta, in the Crimea. There were many stops, at Suchumi,

Sochi, Gagry, Novorissisk, and in most of them there was time to go ashore and explore. All along this coast great sanatoria and rest houses had been built for workers from mines, railways and various factories and they were really good, with medical services where required. Yalta had a lot of them and I stayed here for a few days, exploring all the surrounding countryside, by organized trips and on my own. I was even introduced to bathing in the nude, the only kind of bathing the Russians understood then, and very pleasant it was, on that wide sunny beach.

I sailed on to Odessa, had a couple of days there, went to Sevastopol and then by train up to Kiev. This was a magnificent city, with many historical buildings, but alas, it was largely destroyed during the war. Kiev was my last place in the Soviet Union, a pleasant finish to a most exciting trip, and now I faced a problem. I had to get all my films out of the Soviet Union, and legally. I had no intention of trying to do any smuggling. Indeed, I had no need to, for as far as I knew I had not taken any photographs of forbidden subjects and I did not want to compromise any possibilities of a return visit in future years. But what would the officials on the border think?

I worked until nearly 3 a.m. on my final night, developing the last of my films. There followed a long, all-day train journey across the flat plains of the Ukraine. In the late afternoon, at Shepetovka, on the Polish border, a policeman went through every one of my films, looking at each negative. I really think that the negatives were too small for him to see the subjects properly. But he had a job to do and he was quite friendly. To my great relief he passed the lot and I was free to take my precious negatives out of the Soviet Union. It was so easy it seemed almost like an anticlimax.

I stopped off for a few days in Warsaw, where I picked up an excellent guide who showed me all over the city. Then I went on to Berlin, just as the 1936 Olympic Sports were starting. I had not planned to be there on that date, nor was I particularly interested in the sports. It was really rather a nuisance as I would have preferred to see Berlin in a normal state, not all dressed up for this big occasion. But here I met Willson Woodside again and we had a lot to talk about. He was most interested to hear how I had got on since I left Canada and he gave me much good advice. He was a good friend and a most useful one in those early days.

In Berlin I went to the Ministry of Propaganda, as I had a number of questions to ask, and I also wanted to visit a Labour Camp. While waiting for an interview I got talking to two young English men who were also waiting. One turned out to be Beverley Nichols and I went out to a Labour Camp with him the next day. I photographed him with some of the young Germans at the camp and these pictures were used later on in the British press to illustrate the articles he wrote about Germany. The other man was Barrington-Hudson, a somewhat outrageous extrovert but a man I took to right away. We went round quite a lot together in Berlin and I saw him on various occasions back home in England. Later, he was to prove very useful indeed, after the war started.

I went home again and fixed up a room as a study. My parents were very good to me, and made me welcome for as long as I wanted to stay. I put my pictures together and started to write articles. Before I went to Russia, I had been able to see the publicity manager of Ilford Limited. I told him I was just beginning, that I had enough faith in myself to believe I should make a success of photo-journalism, and asked them if they could let me have film for the trip at a favourable price. All I could promise was that, if I was successful, I would mention their film as often as possible. We had a long talk and in the end they gave me all the film I required for the entire trip.

When I returned from the Continent I had no darkroom and so I asked Ilfords if they could make some prints for me. This they did readily, hundreds of prints altogether and to this day I have never had a bill. Ilford had a reputation for helping beginners and I am sure it paid off in the end. Certainly I have always had a warm feeling towards them, and for many years we co-operated together very pleasantly, as this story will reveal. Later, when I had established myself, I had equally pleasant relations with Kodaks, and indeed, I owe a great deal to both these companies for their help and co-operation over many years.

I wrote articles for papers I already knew, and tried out some others as well. For several months I sweated away, turning out as much material as I could. I converted my den at home into a darkroom and made extra prints as required. Soon I began to achieve successes. The *Manchester Guardian* published two or three articles, with pictures, and also the *Manchester Evening News*. *Saturday Night* took two long illustrated features, as promised, and photographic magazines here and in America took several articles. My farming magazine in Canada also took a few, so that before long I was beginning to think that my gamble was coming off.

Subjects on which I wrote articles that sold, sometimes more than once, were:
The Soviet Union in general.
The Caucasus, a former colonial region.
Children in the Soviet Union.
Traffic regulations.
Railways.
Collective farms.
Religion in the Soviet Union.
Moscow.
Photography in the Soviet Union.

I had to do a lot of research and reading-up on many of these subjects, then by adding my own experiences, I was able to write quite authoritative articles. *The Motor,* for instance, carried a long article with twelve pictures on traffic conditions in Russia. There was not much traffic then but the Soviets were planning for the days when there would be, widening streets, making regulations, putting up signs and generally planning to avoid congestion such as was becoming a real menace in other countries. Years later I went back to the Soviet Union and I was able to see how these plans had worked out, because by then there was a lot of traffic. *The Motor* eagerly took another long article, with many new pictures, on Soviet traffic problems and how they were being solved.

I also sold single pictures here and there, and a few for advertising. A man I had met in Russia wrote a long article for *The Times* on his observations there, and he told the editor I had taken pictures at the same time. The result was that one Saturday the famous back page of *The Times,* all pictures, was almost entirely covered with my photographs. I seized every opportunity like this and tried to make the best of each one, as well as thinking out all sorts of ways in which I could get my material published. Indeed, this is essential in one's early days. No one knows you and so you must get out and bcome known. Later, if you are lucky, the world, or at least a small part of it, might come to you for pictures.

I seem to be lucky in the people I meet on my trips. Guy Philips, the journalist on the SIBIR was one. As we talked on the boat, and later on in Moscow, he asked me what I was going to do when I got back. He never had the slightest doubt that I would be successful, apparently. I told him that I must eventually move to London, as my parents' home in Cheshire was too far from journalistic circles to be my permanent address.

'Come and live with me,' he said. 'I've got a small flat and there are two beds. You can pay me ten shillings a week rent, unless you are broke and then we'll forget about it, and we will share the cost of food.'

I made several short trips to London while I was so busy writing articles at home, and saw more than ever how essential it was to live there. So eventually I went and stayed with Guy for more than a year, until he married a girl from Yorkshire, where he came from. Betty often came to the flat, where we gave her a great welcome and then gently pushed her into the kitchen so that she would cook a meal for us! She and I were becoming very friendly and we went everywhere together. In those early day she always insisted on going Dutch treat when we ate out. She was a good sport and gave me a lot of encouragement.

I met a photographic agent in London, who saw my pictures and offered to sell them for me on the usual fifty-fifty basis. He had wide connections, not only in Britain but on the Continent as well. It seemed a good idea and I agreed, subject to retaining my already established markets myself. An agent takes fifty per cent of fees received, but he does all the work—printing pictures, sending them out and so on. Not all his attempts are successful and his expenses can be quite high, so half the fees received is not really excessive. If an agent is any good he will sell far more pictures than a freelance alone could do. I decided to give it a try. I had done about all I could myself; if he could sell more pictures, all the better. It would cost me nothing.

He was interested in my Canadian pictures as well as those of the Soviet Union, and he talked about my doing more travelling. Actually he did quite well for me, on this material and later. But I found an agent was a mixed blessing. One is very much tied and cannot do as much on one's own. Eventually I visualized having my own business complete, and then I would not need an agent. But this was a useful move at the time and I do not regret it.

CHAPTER THREE

The Balkans

Soon afterwards I met someone who had been in the Balkans for some time and he aroused my enthusiasm for going there. My agent was so keen that he offered to pay half the expenses, as long as he had the exclusive rights to sell my pictures. I was more or less broke all through these early times, hence this seemed like a good idea, and so it turned out. I went off to Bulgaria, armed only with a letter of introduction from the Bulgarian Legation in London.

I spent some three months in Bulgaria, travelling all over the country and loving every bit of it. It was a cheap country. I had a room in a small but quite new hotel in Sofia for half a crown per night. I made a point of never paying more than one shilling for a meal. I got a fify per cent reduction on trains, as a foreign visitor, and travelled on them extensively.

It sounds quite incredible now, but my total expenses on this trip, including getting to and from Bulgaria, were just under £100, my share being less than £50.

I walked a lot and hired a bicycle for one trip into the mountains of Macedonia. This part of the country is so hilly that I found I was walking, and pushing the bike, as much as I was riding it. I spent nights in peasant houses, in monasteries and in mountain huts. It was all a grand bit of adventure and I revelled in it. I made a number of good friends, one or two of whom I still see from time to time. And I took hundreds of photographs, again building up stories as I had done in Russia.

I met an American who was doing a thesis on Bulgarian village life. He had chosen a village called Dragalevtsy and he took me to it on several occasions. It was just what I wanted. I took lots of pictures of Bulgarian village life, including a wedding and various other special occasions. My friend was delighted and I later sent him a selection of the pictures to help him illustrate his thesis. The priest who conducted the wedding was a keen photographer himself and he helped me to get pictures of it, even holding up the ceremony now and then to give me a chance.

I became friendly with Charles Stirling, now Sir Charles, then first secretary at the British Legation in Sofia. He told me a lot about Bulgaria and gave me some useful introductions. We went together to the famous Rila Monastery, in the heart of the Rila Mountains, and stayed there, in the monastery itself, as the guests of the chief monk, for a few days. I did a big coverage of the whole life of the monastery and this sold well later on. It is a most colourful place, and occupies a prominent place in the history of Bulgaria. It is always said that, during the five

15

centuries of Turkish rule and oppression, the spark of Bulgarian culture was kept alive in Rila Monastery.

One subject that I knew would make a good story, even before I went to Bulgaria, was rose oil. This small Balkan country produces most of the world's supply of this essential oil, the base of most high quality perfumes, and I was going to be there in May, when the roses were in flower. Here again I was lucky, for I met a delightful young man from Yardley's who was there to buy rose oil. He was going to travel all over the famous Valley of Roses, visiting nearly every distillery, and he suggested that I go with him. How could I ask for anything better? It was a delightful experience and I finished up with a big set of pictures on every aspect of the rose oil business.

I met a Bulgarian journalist, by name Choukanov, and we became good friends. He came out with me quite a lot and was most helpful. We used to sit in the coffee houses in Sofia in the evenings, where all kinds of plots and intrigues were hatched out. He and his journalistic friends would point out to me some of the notorious characters, and occasionally they would suddenly change the subject of conversation as someone whom they suspected sat down near us, doubtless to hear what we were up to. Bulgaria was, in those days, very much of a minor police state and politics were a dangerous game. Quite a few of the men there had been to prison for their political activities. Sofia gaol was known as the University of Democracy, and not without reason.

One day my friends told me that I was under suspicion, so they had heard, because I was a foreigner and seemed to be staying there a long time. It was suggested, apparently that I might be, among a variety of things, connected with the I.M.R.O., a Macedonian revolutionary organization. I was alarmed and said I had better do something about it.

'Don't,' they said. 'It would lower your prestige if they thought you really were only a journalist.'

Choukanov and I went to Samokov for a few days. From there we climbed far up Musalla, the highest mountain in the Balkans. We spent a night in a mountain hut, but got up at about 3 a.m. to climb to the summit in time to see the sun rise. Hundreds of people were doing the same thing, and the trail to the summit sparkled with lanterns and torches as the climbers struggled upwards.

From Samokov Chouky, as I called him, took me to a village where we met the mother of Georgi Dimitrov, the man who defied Goering at the Reichstag fire trial and later became Secretary of the Comintern. He was at that time an exile from his native land, living in Moscow. His mother, a dear old peasant soul of seventy-seven, told me much about her famous son and of the trial. She had been there throughout the whole trial and had gone to Moscow with her son afterwards. They wanted her to stay there but she yearned for her own home and country. Curiously enough, despite this strong communist connection, neither she nor her family had ever been troubled in any way by the Bulgarian authorities. I took several photographs of her sitting in her garden.

Other subjects I covered in Bulgaria included Turks, of which there were many still living there. I got one set of pictures of them emigrating to Turkey, from Varna, a port on the Black Sea coast, though as families they had probably lived in Bulgaria for centuries. I went to Koprivchitsa, a strange almost deserted town in the Sredna Gora Mountains. It used to be the centre of a prosperous wool weaving industry that thrived mightily during the digging of the Suez Canal. These wool merchants sold vast quantities of their thick hand-woven woollen cloth to the Italian workers on the canal. With their new-found wealth they built beautiful wooden houses, with much elaborate carving. But modern textile machinery put them out of business, and only a few of their houses had been saved by wealthy people buying them as country homes. I stayed in one of them that was beautifully restored, and furnished in the old traditional style.

I went off up into the mountains to see a strange tribe of nomads known as the Kara Kachani, who came up from the plains of northern Greece each summer to graze their vast flocks of sheep in the mountain pastures. They built beautifully domed huts of tree branches and spent months up there, making cheese from sheep's milk in immaculate little dairies. Their dogs were so fierce that each one of us in our little party had to have a guard armed with a heavy stick to keep the brutes from biting us. These people wore most elaborate costumes and altogether this made an excellent photographic subject.

My friend Choukanov came with me on several of these trips. We got hot and dusty in the Balkan summer and he was always bathing. At nearly every stream we came to he would strip off and duck into the water naked. I took one or two pictures of him standing nude in rural settings and sold them later to a nudist magazine.

One great advantage of having an agent at this stage of my career was that he continued to make sales while I was away. Otherwise my absence would have meant that nothing was being done to expand my business. After my return home he made up a number of sets of pictures on various Bulgarian subjects, while I wrote suitable articles. Sales were not as easy to make as on the Soviet Union, as Bulgaria was not as newsworthy. But over the next twelve months we did quite well. For instance, pictures with or without articles on Rila Monastery sold in Holland, Germany, Australia, South Africa, India, Canada and in the *Geographical Magazine* in England.

The Rose Oil Industry sold, with long articles, to two magazines in England, and sets of pictures to various foreign countries. I wrote motoring articles, each slanted differently, for *The Motor, Austin Magazine* and the *Ford Times*. I also succeeded in having four photographic articles published in various magazines. *Life Magazine* took several pictures on Dimitrov's mother, at far higher fees than were paid in England. I had three articles published on fishing, one in Switzerland, and this subject has sold a number of times since then. Then followed one on cycling and two on railways, and many individual pictures, at home and abroad. Many more sales were made by me after the war, when Bulgaria came once more into the news. So altogether this was a good investment, and having an agent at that time was very well worth while.

During the following winter I took a series of photographs of the birth of a butterfly. I borrowed chrysalids from the insect man at London zoo, hatching them out in my room by applying gentle heat to them, which they imagined was spring sunshine. They obligingly broke out of their winter homes, their wings quickly expanded and hardened and I photographed the whole intriguing process. I returned the butterflies to the zoo, where they were released into their appropriate cages, and no one lost anything. I gained some interesting sets of pictures which sold quite well over a long period.

I also had a trip on a submarine for a day from Portsmouth, and used flash to get a set of pictures on life inside it. This also sold a few times here and abroad. In the early spring I went to the Scilly Isles to photograph the flower industry and the islands in general. But I went at a time of wild gales and came away with few pictures. That was a lesson in how weather can make a trip a virtual failure, something the freelance must always allow for. It is often heart-breaking, especially when time is short and expenses go on relentlessly. At some stage one must be prepared to cut one's losses.

I was not entirely happy with my agent and felt that he could be more aggressive in his sales attempts. I thought he tended to wait too much for editors to come to him, instead of going out after them. It might have been my own impatience, but anyway, when another agent, a very nice fellow who inspired me immediately, offered to organize photographic subjects and help me to travel more widely, I decidd to give it a try. I was not bound indefinitely to my first agent, only for the photographs I had taken up to that time. He did not like it but he had to put up with it.

My new agent was a succes from the word go. He was so full of ideas for subjects that would make an interesting series of photographs that I had a hard job keeping up with him. One thing that made life much easier for me was that, after we had worked together for a short time and it was obvious that things were going well, he offered to give me a retainer of a few pound per week, enough for my simple living expenses, the amount to be deducted from commissions he would earn for me. Now I did not have to worry about where my next meal would come from or whether I could pay the rent for my room. I was making progress financially but was still a long way from enjoying any sort of satisfactory stable income.

I was by now doing quite a lot of lecturing to photographic societies all over the country, with slides that I made from my own photographs. These lectures were sponsored by Ilford Limited, who paid me a fee and all expenses and the societies got the lectures for nothing. I had started this after my Russian trip and found that lecturing came easily to me. In fact, I quite enjoyed it, despite cold hotels and often cold trains in those far-off days. It was a useful extra source of income and of course I did not have to share this with my agent. It was this lecturing, together with articles I wrote for various photographic magazines, that brought my name in front of a small section of the public but a section that continually expanded. Very useful it was, but I hardly felt that I had earned it at that time.

Just as I was wondering where to go the following summer, 1938, a journalist friend of mine by the name of Philip Saint suggested a trip in his Morris 8 car to other parts of the Balkans. He had just finished a job and wanted to do something interesting before he looked for another. Czechoslovakia was very much in the news at that time, and Rumania sounded interesting. So we decided to go to both these countries and to have a look at Hungary on our way back. We asked the A.A. for information on these countries, but they had very little. They did not disguise their conviction that we were quite mad to think of such an ambitious trip in so small a car. That was just the sort of encouragement we needed. We would share the expenses of the car, food and accommodation, but Philip insisted that if the car broke down or needed big repairs, it would be his responsibility. He had a small tent and we planned to camp out a lot of the time.

We could not leave before the beginning of June. In May of that year a crisis blew up over the Sudeten region of Czechoslovakia, the part along the German frontier. It quietened down and we decided to have a look at that first. We doubted if we would be allowed into that territory but to our surprise we had no trouble at all. I had asked the *Geographical Magazine* in London if they would like a story and pictures on Sudetenland. The answer was an emphatic yes, 'but you'll never be allowed to do it', they said. Well, we did do it.

We travelled all over this picturesque but troubled countryside and we took pictures of everything. Somehow we managed to interview all the main political parties, and got each one of them to show us around. We even had a photographic interview with Henlein himself. We played canny politically. We listened to all that was said, heard all the widely divergent opinions, and just took it all in, only asking questions. These people were all a bit puzzled, expecting us to take sides. But we didn't, and so they went on showing us more and more, which was just what we wanted. I developed my films and sent all the negatives back to my new agent, with full captions, and he submitted a good cross-section of prints to the *Geographical Magazine*. They published them immediately and were delighted with them. They felt they had got a real scoop.

We then went on more leisurely to Prague, a really lovely old city, where we spent several days. Then eastwards across Bohemia, into Slovakia and on to Ruthenia, a very picturesque mountainous province that was then part of Czechoslovakia, though now it is included in the Soviet Union. At Zlin, a strangely modern town in the midst of the Slovakian countryside, we took photographs in the Bata shoe factory and of the garden city which this enterprising firm had built up. We climbed up into the High Tatra Mountains, on the border with Poland and got lost in the clouds. Just in time we came upon a mountain hut where we spent the night with a noisy but friendly crowd of mostly young people, with heat and food to keep us alive. Next morning the clouds had gone and we found we were in the most dramatic mountain scenery, with precipices all round us.

Ruthenia was delightful, quiet and peaceful, largely forested and it seemed very remote. But it was also a potential trouble spot and did, in fact, finish up with a political crisis of its own, all part of Nazi Germany's expansion in Europe, of course. My pictures came in very useful later on.

By now we were having trouble through constantly breaking springs on our car. The roads were often bad, full of pot holes and, indeed, springs became our chief worry from now on. But to our delight we found that virtually every blacksmith, even in remote villages could make new leaves and fit them. They were used to it with their own local cars. In one village the blacksmith worked all night making new springs, so that we could proceed next morning. He took us to a cottage nearby where a motherly old soul put us up for the night and fed us, asking very little for it all. The blacksmith only wanted a few shillings for his work.

We went on into northern Rumania after Ruthenia. It was similar mountainous country, very beautiful and wild, with primitive villages but the most glorious painted churches, covered all over with frescoes depicting scenes from the Bible. Late on our first afternoon we gave a lift to a young school teacher to a nearby village. It resulted in us spending the night in the Primaria, the council chamber of the village, really just one room in one of the larger houses. We were a sensation. It seemed as though the whole village gathered round to watch us spread out our sleeping bags on the floor and cook a meal on our primus stove. They were still there when we wanted to turn in. The only way to get rid of them, nice friendly people though they were, was to start undressing. Then, with screams from the women and girls, the whole crowd melted away and we spent a peaceful night. They were all back again before we woke up in the morning.

In northern Rumania I did a bit of spying, yes, real spying. In England there were stories about a secret railway that the Rumanians had built so that Soviet troops could go to the aid of Czechoslovakia if she was attacked by the Nazis. We decided to try and find it. Some hikers who spoke a little English told us exactly where it was, so we went to see for ourselves. The story in an English newspaper stated that it was a brand new four-track railway line. This sounded highly improbable, but we did find the railway. It was a single line but obviously new and well made, with heavy rails. We actually walked along it and took photographs, and there was no one there to stop us. One man walking along the line greeted us as though it was quite natural for two Englishmen with cameras to be walking along this new and secret line.

Later on I wrote an article on this and sent it out to a London newspaper. But here I came upon the equivalent of a 'D' notice. The British Government knew something of this line and for their own good reasons did not want it to be publicised. The newspapers were asked not to publish any story about it that might turn up. As the Nazi-Czech crisis was blowing up again, and Lord Runciman was then in Prague, they obeyed. My story was eventually published in one paper and created a certain amount of interest, though it was really too late. If I had been earlier with it, I wonder if I might have affected history in any way. That is the only spying I have ever done, though all foreign correspondents and journalists are believed to do some, from time to time. The Foreign Office have never asked me!

In Rumania we camped out a lot but it got us into trouble with the police or the military. It seemed that camping by foreigners in those days was a highly suspicious act. Hence we were frequently woken in the middle of the night to find a ring of armed police and soldiers round us, pointing rifles at us. This meant getting up and dressing and being taken along, usually with our car, to some nearby police station and handed over to the police. There, what with language difficulties, it was a problem indeed to prove that we were really quite harmless. But we were never thrown into gaol and alway managed to be released in the end. It became a routine and a very tedious one.

On one occasion, late at night, I fell asleep while being questioned in a police station, to everyone's sheer astonishment. In another one the police chief was roaring drunk. He waved away the soldiers, who had arrested us for camping too near a guarded bridge, gave us a hearty greeting and a drink and then let us go, but warned us to camp further away from the bridge.

We were even arrested in the main square of Cernowitz, in broad daylight, and taken to the police station. Our crime apparently consisted of taking photographs in a border region, the border in this case being some forty miles away. I happened to know that the manager of one hotel spoke English and I was allowed to go and find him. He could explain our situation better than we could. I had to leave Philip as hostage, and also my camera with the railway pictures in it. The manager turned out to be a friend of the police chief and he soon got us out of trouble, or nearly. The police insisted on developing Philip's film and we had to wait for two days so that they could see if there was anything incriminating on it. They had not actually seen me take any pictures and I swore that I had not done so. So my film was safe, I hoped.

The hotel manager came out with an excellent idea.

'Come and stay in my hotel,' he said. 'I will let you have a room at a special rate, and tomorrow I will take you out for the whole day into Bessarabia. You will see a lot of interesting things there.'

We had decided against doing this because we heard that the roads were terrible. But he told us that they were quite good and it would be well worth while. We gladly accepted his offer.

He was as good as his word, a most excellent guide. We drove as far as the Soviet border, even managing to take pictures, despite this really being a border region. Our guide knew the military commander at Hotin, on the frontier, who readily gave us permission to use our cameras. We could see big collective farms on the other side of the River Dneister, quite a contrast to the primitive farming in Bessarabia. It was after dark when we returned to Cernowitz, but we had had a really splendid day. I secured pictures which came in very useful later on, when the war started.

Next day we received Philip's film from the police and we were ushered out of the town in a most friendly way. I could not send my railway film home in case the package was opened, though as soon as possible I developed it. That was a rather narrow squeak.

In Bukarest, the Ministry of Tourism, to whom we had a letter of introduction from London, took us under their wing. They installed us in a hotel and they wined and dined us in the city. They took one look at our battered little car—it had more broken springs and was covered with mud—and they spirited it away, had it repaired and fully serviced, even washed and polished. And all this on the State. They paid for everything and even gave us a useful amount of pocket money to spend.

They said they wanted us to see more of their country and offered us free rail tickets anywhere, and steamer tickets on the Danube, and they supplied us with petrol coupons for the rest of our trip, which meant free petrol. After a few days in Bukarest, we went by train to Galatz, then down the Danube by ship to Valcov, a curious little town in the delta. Valcov is known as the Venice of Rumania, all canals and hardly any streets. The people there were the descendants of the Old Believers who had fled from religious persecution in Russia in 1815. They still spoke Russian and they had a fine Russian church.

After our return to Bukarest, we were invited to join a very select party of cabinet ministers and other high dignitaries to go down to Curtea de Arges, for a special service in honour of the famous Queen Marie of Rumania, who had recently died. We went by special train, with an excellent breakfast on the way there and a perfectly splendid meal on the way back. I was able to photograph King Carol and Prince Michael at quite close range and we met many of the cabinet ministers.

Above all, we wanted to reach the Black Sea, so we set off in our car across the Dobrudja for Constantsa. We camped out again, sleeping in the open without our tent, but now we had a letter from the Ministry saying that we were allowed to camp if we wanted to. We were still woken up by the police on some nights but the letter worked and we were allowed to stay where we were.

'But why do you want to sleep here in the fields?' they asked us. 'There is a nice inn in the village.'

They just could not understand us but at least they left us alone. One dawn, just before the sun came up, I awoke to hear the sound of wild geese winging overhead to the Danube marshes. At the same time, about two hundred yards away, a man rode by on a horse. He wore a tall fur hat and a wide flowing cloak but his horse made no sound in the soft earth. He never cast a glance our way but just disappeared over a rise in the ground, without a sound. I wonder to this day if I really saw a man and horse of flesh and blood on that strangely beautiful morning when the wild geese heralded the dawn over the Dobrudja.

We stayed on the Black Sea coast near Mamaia for several days, bathing, basking in the hot sun and generally relaxing. For this was our furthest point and from here on we should be homeward bound. In Bukarest we collected a wad of petrol coupons, bade farewell to our friends at the Tourist Ministry and set off northwards into the mountains of Transylvania. At Campina we contacted one of the oil companies and they gave us a guide who took us in his own car over typical parts of the Rumanian oil fields and refineries. I took lots of pictures and, in view of the forthcoming war, this later turned out to be one of the most useful subjects I have ever photographed. One picture alone, of oil derricks, was probably reproduced more than fifty times, all over the world. Few people had any pictures of these oil fields. I gave a set to the Foreign Office when the war started, and for all I know they may have been useful.

Transylvania is very beautiful and we lingered amidst its wooded mountains for several days, then crossed the border into Hungary.

'Back in civilization again,' said Philip. 'Now we can proceed like free citizens instead of suspected criminals.'

But how wrong he was. We camped in the late afternoon among some small haystacks and were in the middle of our meal when once again we were surrounded by armed soldiers, this time in daylight. Their officer spoke French and I was able to gather that, incredibly, we had camped in the midst of army manoeuvres. This was the worst arrest of the lot and it took us until well after midnight to get free, although our innocence must have been apparent to all. In the end we insisted that they put us up for the night in a police station, as we could not find another more suitable campsite in the dark. They looked quite dumbfounded but they did put us up, and even gave us breakfast in the morning. They posted an armed man in our room throughout the night.

We loved Budapest, with its many fine bridges across the Danube and the old buildings on the slopes of the Buda side. Here Philip and I parted company. He was going down into Italy to meet his fiancée and to take her home. So I went off on my own by train into the Puszta, the great plains in the north-east of the country, where vast herds of cattle and sheep are guarded by shepherds in strange costumes. Horsemen, splendid riders on superb animals, rounded up the cattle, huge long-horned white beasts that all looked like prize animals to me.

I went on by train to Prague for a couple of days. On our way through Prague earlier I had been to see a friend at the British Legation, and had mentioned the secret railway in Rumania. He said they had heard about it but did not really think that it existed. But if I found it, they would be interested to know. I was now able to tell him that we had indeed found it, and photographed it. He was staggered and told me that, in the meantime, they had made further inquiries and decided that the mysterious railway really had not been built. It is no exaggeration to say that my news electrified him.

'You should employ a good amateur spy now and then,' I remarked, rather cruelly. He offered to send the pictures home for me, in the diplomatic bag, but I declined. He was really worried when I told him I was going home through Germany, and he begged me to go by some other route. I did not have enough money for that and in any case I did not see what the Germans could do if they found some railway pictures among my many negatives. They were not to know where the pictures had been taken. I had no trouble whatever, of course, and was soon home again quite safely.

I found on my return that I was really making some progress. Stories I had done in England before I left were selling, my agent had a long list of features for me to do and, of course, I had all the new material from the trip I had just completed. There were requests for many more lectures during the coming winter, so I was going to be busy. Quite a few good sales had been made of my Sudeten pictures; Czechoslovakia was always in the news and many of my photographs took on the aspect almost of news pictures. The *Geographical Magazine* actually used twenty of them and many were sold in Australia, as my agent had good connections there. The prices were not as good as in Britain but they all added up.

Ruthenia came into the news in late 1938 when Hungary and Poland were threatening to snatch it from the weakened Czechoslovakia. A motoring magazine had somewhat reluctantly taken an article from me on this remote province and the very day it was published there were headlines in all the daily papers about Ruthenia. The editor phoned me to say how delighted he was that I had handed him a scoop.

Rumania as a whole remained a good subject for a long time, as it was always coming into the news. The oil fields particularly were of great interest, especially as Hitler began to penetrate the country economically, and I made a real killing later on when the Nazis marched into Rumania. The editor of an oil magazine asked me to write a long article on the oil fields, their productive possibilities and the prospects of the Germans moving large quantities of oil up into central Europe.

Without being able to use sea-borne transport, the Nazis were actually very much hampered, as railways and the Danube together could not possibly move anything like the whole output. Only if the Germans were fighting near the oil fields would they be really useful, and then of course they might be destroyed in the fighting. I had to do a lot of research on this subject, and learn the language of the oil business, but the article was published and I was well paid for it. Years later, when the retreating German armies fell back on Rumania from Russia, I sent out my oil pictures again and made some further sales. I had almost an exclusive on the subject.

I wrote several motoring articles after this long trip, not about the whole journey but splitting it up into 'Motoring in Ruthenia', 'With a Car in Rumania,' and so on. Philip wrote one he called 'From Battersea to the Black Sea,' and I illustrated it with my pictures. My agent made up sets of pictures on different subjects—we worked them out together—and sometimes he would print a dozen sets. If they would sell in one country, they should sell in others. This is where an agent can be so useful.

I did a lot of photography that winter and into the next Spring. I made a set of pictures on a modern health centre and another on a technical college. I went down to the Cotswolds and took many pictures of the making of billiard cloth at Cam. The mill people were so pleased with the pictures that they asked me to take more, of other cloths, for their own use, a nice little commission. I wrote a long article for the *Geographical Magazine* on the making of billiard cloth.

My agent had a request from Sweden for a set of pictures of the Swedish Legation, with the Minister and his wife. I did this and it sold to two magazines and an evening paper in England as well. A request for a set on the Swedish church in

London followed, another useful job. I went on a press visit to Pilkington's glass works at St. Helens and took some pictures of glass making. Again, the company liked some of them and asked to use them. I went to Ireland for nearly a month and took masses of pictures of all kinds of subjects—Dublin and the country nearby, and I even had a long photographic interview with Dr. Hyde, the President, and another one with Mr. de Valera, who was Prime Minister then.

I went on to Belfast and received valuable help from the Northern Ireland Industrial Development Board, in particular from its director, Robert Frizzell. This led to a long and most pleasant friendship which resulted in several more trips to Northern Ireland after the war. In Ulster I did a lot of industrial photography, all with my Leica, much of it with quick time exposures, a technique which I used a great deal.

So often the lighting on a man or woman at work is good but not strong enough for a hand-held exposure. Rather than spoil the effect, possibly, by using flash, or going to the trouble and often upheaval of using floodlights, I put my camera on a tripod, focused and composed carefully and took perhaps a half or one second exposure at an aperture that would give me enough depth of field. A person can usually keep quite still, and look perfectly natural, for that length of time, when he is concentrating on his work and not looking at the camera. Sometimes I could get quite a number of people to keep still together in a wider factory shot.

In a linen mill, I discovered that the reigning Linen Queen worked there, so I made a set of pictures of her at work and in her home. There was a good market for that sort of thing in those days, in women's magazines. Today it would not be sophisticated enough! Each evening I developed my films and in the morning I cut them up into strips and put them away before I went out to do another day's work.

My agent looked after all the work involved with these many different stories, having the prints made, putting the right captions on them and sending them out to prospective markets. Without an agent, I would have had to do all this myself, taking up much of my time and probably involving me in considerable expense. Instead, I prepared to do more photography and planned more travelling.

CHAPTER FOUR

The Year of the War

Early in 1939 I was invited to join a press party visiting Zurich, in Switzerland, my first invitation abroad. It was the occasion of the Swiss National Exhibition, an event which takes place every twenty five years, but in a different city each time. This gave me a lasting impression of how well the Swiss organize things, how thorough, painstaking and experienced they are—in other words, how civilized, in the best sense of the word. The exhibition was most impressive, laid out beautifully along the lake shore, with exhibits of every conceivable kind. They even had an armaments section, with notices to the effect that photography was *not* forbidden.

We had an interview with the Swiss President, and I took a number of candid pictures of him, trying to be unobtrusive. I used my tripod and took exposures of half a second, choosing moments when he was still, and I ended up with a good variety of attitudes and expressions. We also went out into the Jura Mountains to see some very noisy and realistic army exercises. Again, I was allowed to take photographs of everything.

I took advantage of being in Switzerland to stay on and see more of the country. At that time, though, I did not think such a well known and much photographed country would be much use to me. I thought it had been done to death. How wrong I was! We did quite well with the pictures I took, but since the war I have been back many times and Switzerland has, indeed, turned out to be one of the most successful of the many countries we have photographed. Probably just because it is so popular.

My agent had some good connections in Italy and Germany, and he also had money in both countries which he could not get out. He suggested that I go to both countries, use up some of his money, make use of the people he knew there, and try to get some good stories. It seemed obvious that war was going to break out later that year, so these two countries were at least topical. Betty came out to Switzerland after the press party had gone home, for her holiday, and we wandered round parts of Switzerland together and then went down into Italy.

The Swiss people gladly gave us railway tickets and put us up in hotels. We went to Lucerne, to Einsiedeln Monastery and to Winterthur, where I did some photography in the big engineering works of Sulzer Brothers. In Italy we stopped off for a couple of days in Bologna and then Florence, before going on to Rome.

We fell in love with these beautiful Italian cities and have never yet fallen out of love with them, despite numerous visits since. All too soon Betty had to go home.

In Rome I did stories on the Vatican, on Rome in general, by day and night, and on the Forum, recently very much excavated by Mussolini. I took pictures in the Capucine Church vaults, of the countless skeletons and human bones, giving exposures of sixty seconds in the rather dim light. I went to the Fascist Party headquarters and asked them for help. I did not commit myself politically at all. I hated the fascist and nazi régimes and all they stood for—but I asked them to show me what they were doing to make life better for their people. They gave me a guide, a charming young aristocrat married to an English girl, and we went everywhere.

I did stories on a home for unmarried mothers, on a wonderful creche —'Musso's Bonny Babies'—, on the brand new Foro Mussolini, a splendid sports centre, and on a big T.B. hospital, to mention only a few subjects. I managed to get a photographic interview with Signor Gayda, 'Mussolini's Mouthpiece', as he was known, a most cordial and unassuming man who did everything I wanted in the way of posing. I tried to get another interview with Count Ciano, the Foreign Minister, but it seemed to be so difficult that in the end I gave up and went off to Munich. A few days after I had left he said he would be glad to see me. It was too late.

In Munich the Nazi Party did a lot to help me. I was invited to various functions, in one of which I was able to 'shoot' Hitler and Goering and other big Nazis from reasonable range with a telephoto lens. I had an interview with Gauleiter Wagner, in his office in Munich, and there met Hoffman, Hitler's personal photographer, who claimed to have a hundred thousand photographs of the Fuehrer. He kindly allowed me to use his lights, which were already set up.

I bought a bicycle and went off into the beautiful Bavarian countryside, to Garmisch and Füssen and some of the famous castles. The Nazi Party put me up in a hotel in Füssen and I went out with parties of workers from Essen on Kraft durche Freude trips, in buses, to Mittenwald and Oberammergau and many other lovely places. I took pictures of how the German workers enjoyed themselves as a reward for good work done in their factories.

Everyone said there would be war soon, but not until the harvest was in. So I kept my eye on the cornfields and decided I would go home when the corn turned yellow and was being cut. I met an old lady in a pension where I stayed. She was skilful as an astrologist and had worked out, with much trouble and time, Hitler's horoscope. She said it was necessary to know the exact time of a person's birth to get a horoscope right. She had worked out Hitler's and she said that war would start in Poland in six week's time from then. She was exactly right, to the day. But by then I was safely home. Some of my stories sold; others were rendered useless by the war starting too soon. But it was all valuable experience and many of my pictures sold later on.

The war started but nothing much happened in the way of fighting for some months. But everything was blacked out and life began to get difficult in a number of ways. I offered my services as a photographer or writer to the Ministry of Information but they did not want to know me. I offered to join the Forces, but was told I was too old then. I must wait until I was called up. So I got busy doing feature stories on war subjects. I had to have a M.O.I. permit to take photographs at all. For entry into special areas I had to have an extra pass for each job. They were not hard to get.

I did a number of trips, with other members of the press, to barrage balloon sites, to watch various kinds of troop training, to the Observer Corps, the Engineers, School of Cookery, Eton College boys doing war work on the land (one of them asked me to show him how to light a bonfire), evacuated children, pets in war time, the various women's services—A.T.S., W.A.A.F., W.R.N.S., and the police force. Many of these features appeared in women's magazines, especially one, now defunct, which used much of my work, and they also sold abroad.

I went up to Tyneside and did a big story on the revival of industry on that recently depressed area. I had to have a special permit to go into munitions works, aircraft factories, steel works and so on, and all my pictures, of course, had to be censored before we could send them out anywhere. On this job I was given a police escort much of the time because so many people reported me for taking photographs.

Soon after the war started Betty and I decided that it was very awkward trying to find each other in the black-out and it would be much nicer if we were married. We had been waiting until our financial position was somewhat more secure, but with a war on there seemed to be no point in waiting. So we got married, quite quietly. We found an attractive modern flat in Hampstead, with central heating, something I just insisted upon as a bare necessity of life after living in Canada, and we settled down very cosily. If we were going to be killed in the war we might as well enjoy life together first.

Thus I kept myself very busy photographically, doing some good, I hoped, by showing the public something of the war effort. My Balkan pictures were selling well, too, as these countries came into the news. I did a lot of lecturing on these same countries, many of them public lectures at quite good fees. These were booked through Christy's Agency, now Foyles, who sent someone to hear one lecture and promptly put me on their lists. I went all over the country, and Ilfords often booked me up for intervening nights if I had several lectures say, in the north of England or the west. Sometimes I lectured for ten nights or so, almost in a row.

I enjoyed lecturing, once I had got used to it. I had suffered agonies the first few times, then realised that, with slides going on all the time, it was not at all difficult. I tried to tell a worthwhile story, including many personal experiences and anecdotes. And I had a few pet jokes which usually produced a laugh. It was shattering when they didn't: I wondered what was wrong! I always tried to speak clearly and loudly enough for everyone at the back of the audience to hear me. I am always dismayed when experienced lecturers fail to cast their voices far enough. I had audiences from a hundred or less to nearly two thousand. I lectured at the Royal Photographic Society several times, before and during the war, and had some afternoon lectures in various places because of the black-out. It was a marvellous experience standing in the lobby of the Bournemouth Pavilion watching people crowding in to hear my lecture and to realize that forty per cent of all the money they were paying in was coming to me.

Then suddenly the phony war was over. Bombing started with a vengeance, my business dropped off, paper became scarce and it was obvious that I could not go on like this much longer. As so often, it seems, in my life, something turned up at the right moment. My friend Barrington-Hudson, whom I had seen on various occasions since first meeting him in Berlin in 1936, phoned me up one day and said that, if I liked to apply to the War Office for a post as official photographer, he would back me up with a personal recommendation. I applied, was called for an interview and there met a major who at first was very grumpy and unfriendly. I had taken a cutting book along with me to show the W.O. what I had been doing photographically. He looked through it casually, then his face lit up.

'Ah,' he exclaimed, 'you have been in Rumania? My second home. I have worked there for years.'

That broke the ice and a little while later I appeared before a selection board and finally had a medical examination. All was well and I was duly called up. But I was in the midst of lectures and other things and had to ask for a week to clear things up. Then I was in the Army. I was kitted out with battle dress and all the bits and pieces, but I was commissioned right away. Official photographers were among the very few people commissioned during the war without any form of training. So on my first day in the Army I became Lieutenant Cash. It was March 3rd, 1941.

CHAPTER FIVE

In the Army

I was posted to the War Office itself for six months, and was able to live at home. All the other photographers were Fleet Street men and I only heard long afterwards that I was very much on trial for the first month. The old hands never thought I could make the grade if I hadn't had newspaper experience. But I knew nothing of this and they were all very decent to me, helping me in a variety of ways. I made many good friends among these veterans and I think I became accepted by them.

I was actually on a civilian contract, as were the other photographers, not on the usual army pay and allowances, and we were in many respects better off that way. Later, when I went abroad, I was much better off, having a foreign allowance as well, and certain income tax benefits. I did not ask for all this; that was the way it worked out for official photographers.

I went out, sometimes with other photographers, all over the country, photographing troops training and on defence duties, building bridges, digging defence works, carrying out exercises, sometimes on a big scale. Once, in East Anglia, during a demonstration of a live barrage, a big shell landed close to me, wounded one man and it might have ended my career then and there. It had fallen short and caused a lot of confusion.

I was often sent out with V.I.P's, including cabinet ministers, the Army Chief Lord Gort (we had an interesting talk about Leica photography, one of his hobbies) and sometimes royalty. I photographed the Queen, now the Queen Mother, so often that she used to recognize me and give me a pleasant smile. The King was difficult to photograph. He did not like it, especially from his left side and once muttered that it would be better from the other side. It was a royal command but I could not get a picture from the other side, so that is one that did not get taken.

Staying at Yarmouth one night, ready for a job the next day, I found I was in the midst of the town's first blitz. It was mostly an incendiary raid. Fire bombs dropped on the hotel and all round; I got dressed and was outside in record time. I spent the whole night photographing the raid, trying not to get hit or burnt, and ended up with some pictures that pleased certain people at the War Office very much. The whole town was on fire and the fire services just could not cope with it at all. Part of the time I was helping to haul hoses around and to carry buckets of water, but it was hopeless.

Then, suddenly, I was posted to the Middle East, at a week's notice. Betty was very distressed but of course we had to accept it. I sailed from Liverpool in a big convoy of troopships and it took us some nine weeks to reach Suez. We crossed the Atlantic almost to Canada at first, then turned south-eastwards to Sierra Leone, in West Africa, on to Cape Town, where we had three marvellous days ashore with wonderful hospitality and entertainment, then up to Suez, and to Cairo by train. During the voyage many of us gave lectures to the troops. I seemed to have the largest number of subjects of anyone on board. I also made a complete set of pictures of life on board a troop ship.

I reported to G.H.Q., Middle East, had a few days in Cairo, then went out to the Western Desert. The war was quite a long way off in those days, more than two days driving, in fact, first along the coast road and then inland into the desert itself. I went out to Army H.Q. with Freddy Bayliss, a Paramount News cameraman who was killed later. He was a great character, a natural extrovert, and completely fearless. He had gone into a tank battle in his soft vehicle, got it shot up and had carried on into the battle clinging to a tank. He showed me how to navigate with a compass across the desert, once we had left the coast road. I had to walk fifty yards in front of the car, take a compass reading on some object in our general direction, perhaps only a big rock or a bush. Then we would drive up to the object and do it all over again. One cannot get an accurate compass reading near to a motor vehicle because of the mass of metal. Hence the necessity of walking away from it.

We came upon Army H.Q., just some tents in the desert wastes, after two and a half days driving. We each had a small tent and a camp bed, with blankets, so we could always kip down anywhere. One night we spent in a cave, out of the cold. For this was December and the weather was quite cold, by day or night. The first man I met at the press camp was Randolph Churchill, then a war correspondent, bashing out a story on a typewriter while sitting in the sun. He got up, introduced himself and showed me round the camp. Other officers turned up later.

The first job I did after settling down out there was to make a set of photographs of a tank hospital, an engineers' camp where tanks were repaired and put back into action. It meant a long drive westwards, through the wire, the huge barbed wire fence that Mussolini had put up all along the Libyan border before the war ever began. I had a small truck with a driver and by mid-morning we had found the camp.

In the western desert there were several main tracks, known by names such as the Axis Track, the Diamond Track, and so on. Each was marked by iron stakes topped by a piece of sheet metal of a certain shape—square, diamond, round, etc., spaced two hundred yards apart. The desert surface was mostly quite hard and stony, the real sand dunes being far away inland. But this hard surface soon got chewed up by heavy traffic, so that drivers tended to keep to the hard surfaces on one side or other of the posts. This went on until one merely followed the masses of tracks in the general direction, rarely catching a glimpse of the iron stakes. In some places a heavily-used track would be as much as seven miles wide, yes, seven miles.

I took my pictures of the tank hospital and a most interesting job it was. At lunch time we were suddenly strafed by ten Messerschmidt 110's, flying very low. Everyone dived into slit trenches but I could not find one. I hid behind a small bush, lying flat on my stomach, and watched the raid. The Germans squirted the whole camp with machine gun fire and dropped a few small bombs. I saw a petrol tanker blow up and one man was badly injured, but they missed me. It was really all over in a few seconds, my first blooding in the desert.

On the way back we drove through a gap in the wire, then turned south. Had we turned north we would have run into the enemy around Halfaya Pass, but more of that later. The wire was a wonderful guide in those days. When you were lost—and that was easy in this vast featureless desert—you always tried to find the wire. Then you knew what to do. It was a strange form of warfare, very fluid, and it was quite easy to run into enemy units on the move, or come up suddenly behind one of their camps. In that case it was the man who got out fastest who survived. Once I ran into shellfire which turned out to be from our own guns. I was behind the enemy and I could see them a mile away on a hillside. I got out fast.

Soon Army H.Q. moved a hundred miles westwards. Our troops had advanced a long way but had left a big concentration of enemy troops on the coast, in Sollum, Bardia and Halfaya Pass. We had to go far inland to avoid these pockets, and come down to the coast beyond them. Vehicles moved in groups, perhaps fifty at a time, each group with a navigating officer. The various trucks took up positions like ships in a convoy and kept in that formation in the swift drive across the open desert, kicking up vast clouds of dust. Few stops were made, but sudden changes of course took place as suspected enemy tanks or guns were seen in the distance. No planes appeared, fortunately.

Around this time, the army photographers were paired up, one cine and one still, with a small truck and a driver. We could go where we liked, our main object being to find the war and photograph it, not always easy to do. We drew rations whenever possible, and petrol, and looked after ourselves entirely, linking up with any units that were going into action or doing anything interesting. I was joined by Arthur Graham, a cine photographer, and we were together for weeks in the desert. We got on well and became good friends.

We were now near the Green Belt, a long stretch of low hills along the coast, scattered with some fine Roman ruins, for this whole region was the granary of Rome two thousand years ago. It was a pleasant change. The harsh desert scenery and the appalling dust were suddenly replaced by rolling green hills, fields and little white farm houses (erected by the Italians for their settlers but now all deserted) and we came upon small towns and villages. Derna was the first.

We went into Derna, right along the main street between the white houses, with bougainvillea draped across the road in full flower, in a convoy of Indian troops who were occupying the town. There were no Italians or Germans left, only the local Arabs and they lined the streets and gave us a great welcome. It all made good pictures. We camped in the house formerly occupied by the Italian General Graziani and very comfortable it was. We were filthy with a month's dust and grime, as we rarely had enough water in the desert to be able to wash, only enough to drink. So off with our clothes and into the cold December sea we dived and it was sheer luxury.

We went forward next day with the advancing troops but were held up by a blown-up road on a steep escarpment. Another chap and myself climbed a hill where there was an observation tower, with views for many miles across the whole countryside. We were the most advanced troops of the whole Eighth Army at that moment, but there was not an enemy in sight. We were the first to enter Barce, the next small town, along with a couple of armoured cars. Again, no enemy troops were there. They had all gone, as well as the civilians, but the Italian police had been left behind to keep order among the Arabs.

These formerly oppressed Arabs were taking it out on the police, teasing them and even trying to grab their rifles. Suddenly one policeman lost his temper and fired into the crowd. A young man standing close to me was shot in the stomach and died horribly in a sea of blood at my feet. There was nothing we could do to help him; he was too badly hurt. Then a few red-caps arrived and stopped the rioting. Again, the Arabs gave us a warm and friendly welcome. One small hotel was still open. The manager said he had no food of any kind but would cook our own for us. He was magnificent and that night we really ate well.

The enemy put up little fight during their big retreat. This was 1941, long before Alamein, of course, and battle fronts were rarely clearly defined. Soon we heard that Benghazi had been evacuated so off we went again, and once more we were among the first handful of troops to enter the town. This is quite a big place and a formal surrender had been arranged somehow. A South African general was to accept the town from the Italian police chief in the main square. We prepared to photograph this momentous occasion. The general arrived. The police chief got out of his car. There was a sudden shot and the police chief fell to the ground. One of his own men, nervous and trigger happy, had accidentally fired his rifle and shot his chief in the leg. And that was the end of the ceremony.

This was Christmas Day and miraculously, in the afternoon, the Christmas treat of turkeys and all sorts of food and drink arrived from our headquarters in Cairo. Our numbers were soon swelled by war correspondents and other army photographers, with their drivers and various camp followers. We occupied a block of modern flats, as their Italian occupiers had fled, leaving all their furniture behind, even cutlery, and that night we had a great feast. The army cooks did us proud and, by tradition, the officers served the men first and we were then served in turn. Afterwards we found a piano in one of the flats and we had an uproarious evening. Richard Dimbleby, of the B.B.C., was there and he performed on the piano magnificently. Some time during the evening there was an air raid, with bombs falling all round us, but no one took the slightest notice. It was a night to remember.

The war stagnated here for a while. Graham and I drove ninety miles westwards along the coast and only knew we had reached enemy territory when our truck was shelled. We turned round and went back; there was no future there. We decided to go back east and look for stories among the Roman ruins at Cirene or further still. Bardia, where the big concentration of enemy troops had been cut off, had just fallen so we went there. The South Africans, established in Bardia, were keeping an eye on the enemy and we joined up with them. A plan was afoot to capture the little village of Sollum, down below on the narrow coastal plain. Halfaya Pass was four miles away along the escarpment and it held thousands of enemy troops. They made no attempt to break out or to raid our tenuous lines, though they far outnumbered us.

One cold windy night Graham and I went down the cliffs with a few hundred of the South Africans, ready for a dawn attack on Sollum. We descended on a narrow and very steep path in the darkness. Collectively, we must have made a frightful lot of noise, but somehow the enemy never heard us. We settled down in a dry wadi a few feet deep to await the dawn. I thought the village might be a quarter of a mile away but as the first light appeared, I discovered that the nearest stone houses were only a hundred yards away, each one full of enemy troops. We had heard some of them moving about in the dark, drawing water from a well somewhere near.

The attack was heralded by a ten minute barrage from our guns hidden a few miles away in the desert. Their firing was, fortunately, most accurate but it woke the enemy up. Our little wadi was soon filled with bursting mortar bombs and fairly sizzling with enemy machine gun fire. The barrage stopped suddenly and the troops went over the top. We two stayed back after photographing them in the dim light, waiting for the enemy to be winkled out of the houses. But it didn't happen that way. Only half the houses were captured. The other half still contained German and Italian troops. There was stalemate, and it lasted all day. We had great difficulty getting out of the wadi and back to the cliffs, dodging snipers' bullets.

Next morning a further attack was made and this was successful. We got close-up shots of the enemy surrendering, being chased out of the houses with hand grenades and generally mopped up. It was a good story, and long afterwards I saw many of my pictures that had been printed in British papers and magazines.

A few days later the enemy surrendered Halfaya Pass. Our little attack on Sollum had cut off their only water supply. Graham and I went in with a dozen or so South African officers and to take the surrender. An Italian soldier with a white flag, led us through a minefield and there we were, barely a score of us facing nine thousand crack German and Italian troops. But everything was most correct. The enemy troops were formed up into long lines, disarmed and marched away through the minefields to temporary prisoner-of-war camps in the desert. We released about a hundred British prisoners and I photographed them watching their former captors being marched away. It was a glorious sunny day, perfectly clear, with the most wonderful views from those high cliffs down on to Sollum and for miles along the coast and across the Mediterranean. We nearly ran out of film, there was so much to photograph.

Our films were normally taken back to Cairo for processing by air or dispatch riders, but now that we were so much nearer to the Nile Valley we decided to take this lot ourselves. We drove for many hours, covering nearly four hundred miles before stopping for the night, and handed in our films in Cairo the next morning. I found that a new job was waiting for me. The War Office had decided to expand our unit by creating an Army Film and Photo Unit, made up of several groups of still and cine photographers, all sergeants, with a lieutenant in charge of each group of six. They were to be attached to divisions and to stay with their own division through thick and thin, and to photograph all their activities. Quite different to the freelance sort of existence I had enjoyed, but it made sense in the changing conditions which developed later. I was to be Picture Editor, in Cairo, selecting and writing up all the pictures taken by the Army photographers. My commanding officer, Colonel Astley, told me about it and then said:

'Allan, I haven't the slightest idea what you are to do. You are supposed to know. We shall soon find out if you are a success by the number of our pictures which are published in the British press.'

I knew what to do, alright. I had apparently been selected for this job because I had done journalistic work as well as photography before joining the War Office. Up to now we had taken pictures mostly with their news value in mind. Now we were to make up features as well, big sets of pictures on definite subjects that would appeal to editors of illustrated papers like *Picture Post, Illustrated* and so on. I would have to organize these features, write them up and send them to London ready to use. All our material was distributed by the Ministry of Information in London, not only to the British press but abroad as well. I would be judged by the amount of extra photographs and feature stories that were published. It was the first time such a post had been created in the British Army anywhere.

My new work was not to start for a month or so, and Colonel Astley asked me to go up to Palestine, Syria and the Lebanon with him. We had photographers stationed in those countries as well and he wanted to visit them. At the same time I could explain the new set-up to them and tell them what to do. I was delighted. I did not like the discomforts of the desert and I relished living clean again.

This trip was just like a holiday for me, new territory to add to my travels. I had taken my Leica with me to the Middle East but I never used it on war subjects. I was paid to do war photography, and all the pictures I took belonged to the War Office. But away from war areas and troops, and in my own time, I began taking Leica pictures just as I had done in the Balkans and elsewhere. I had brought a good supply of Ilford film with me, and developers, my Correx tank, etc. and from now on I began to use them.

We had a staff car and we were to drive first to Jerusalem. It was a long way, over three hundred miles from Cairo. It was a hundred and eighty miles from the Suez Canal, which we crossed on a ferry, to Beersheba, on the far side of the Sinai Desert, the first sign of civilization. My colonel said that we would not need rations because the manager of Shepherd's Hotel, whom he knew well, was supplying us with a picnic lunch. We set off at dawn and about mid-day we pulled off the road on to a hard bit of desert to eat our lunch. It consisted of cold chicken, salad, rolls and butter and grapes, all contained in an ice box. Our driver, the colonel and myself all sat down together on the desert sand and enjoyed it; a meal I shall long remember.

I fell for Jerusalem immediately, especially the old city, with its winding alleys, its holy places, both Christian and Moslem, its teeming people in their colourful costumes and its old mellowed walls and towers. I spent many hours on this occasion, and on future visits, just wandering round everywhere, and invariably got lost. Jerusalem is still one of my favourite cities. We went on to Beirut and over the Lebanon Mountains to the magnificent ruins of Baalbek, then further north through Homs and Hama to Aleppo, coming back down the coast through Tripoli. Colonel Astley returned to Cairo but I stayed on to do some feature stories.

One assignment I was given was to photograph the defences in the hills around Tripoli, being built then in case the Germans invaded Turkey and swept down this coast towards Egypt. Each day I went up into the mountains with one of the Australian officers doing this work. We drove up as far as we could, then got out and scrambled up the slopes. On one occasion we rode on horse-back, all through the olive groves on the lower slopes, amidst great drifts of early Spring flowers, a wonderful sight. I stayed with the Australians for a week; they were a grand bunch of friendly chaps.

I went far up into the Lebanon Mountains to do a story on the Military Ski School, where troops were being trained in mountain warfare on skis. This was at the famous Cedars of Lebanon, almost the only group of these lovely trees left. Cedar wood from near there was taken to build King Solomon's Temple in Jerusalem long centuries ago, but at that time all the slopes were covered with these trees. I got some dramatic pictures of the white-clad troops on skis high up among the rocky peaks.

I did another story on the Indian Mule Corps in the Lebanon Mountains, and another one on a similar mule corps from Cyprus. Then I met an officer in the Officer's Club in Beirut who was with the British Druse Regiment. He was helping to train men of the Druse tribes in modern warfare, with camels and horses, down in the Jordan Valley. This was a ready-made feature story so I went to stay with the Druses for a few days and photographed all their activities. They were grand people.

The training made some excellent pictures and the Druses even organized a camel charge and then a charge of horse troops, kicking up clouds of dust as they tore across the sandy ground. It was an exciting subject, but at last I had to return to Cairo and start my new work. I went back by train from Jerusalem.

I had the usual run of more or less news pictures to sort and edit, especially during the long retreat to Alamein, but I started to get our photographers from all over the Middle East to build up feature stories. I even began one myself in Cairo after a time, when our troops had settled down at Alamein. Actually, we were evacuated to Jerusalem during that crisis, just in case Rommel burst into the Nile Valley, but we returned to Cairo later on, when the battle front became stabilized. Then Monty came out to the Middle East and transformed many things. Vast preparations were made for the great battle which would dislodge the enemy from Alamein and drive him eventually right out of North Africa. We prepared to do a big job of photography when the battle started.

We were now equipped to send pictures by radio to London and New York, and we intended to make this a real event. It was one of my jobs to select the pictures which were suitable for radio transmission so that, when the battle started, we were able to send out half a dozen pictures each night. These appeared in all the British newspapers, and in New York, the following morning, sometimes less than twenty four hours after they had been taken. They were a sensation.

I had anticipated this and had built up a big feature on the work of our own unit, from the photographers in the desert, among the tanks and guns and the dust of earlier battles, to our headquarters, the darkrooms, offices and so on. I even included a picture of myself editing the films! This had all been sent to London in good time so that, when the public began to ask who was responsible for these radio pictures the Ministry of Information was able to send out the whole feature, or individual pictures, of our unit at work. We appeared in almost every magazine and newspaper in the country, and widely abroad as well.

I was extremely busy for a long time after the start of the Battle of Alamein, but it was exciting work. It kept me very much tied to my desk in Cairo, not the best place to be in throughout the hot summers. But eventually, months later, the war moved so far from Cairo, that my job suddenly dried up. Pictures were sent to Algiers, instead of Cairo, and were dispatched to London from there. I was practically unemployed and I asked to be sent home to England. It took months to get any response from the War Office.

A new training magazine was started about this time and I offered to be its official photographer. It was a marvellous job. It took me all over the Middle East again, to training camps of every kind and I filled the new magazine with my pictures, even writing articles in it at times. At the same time I took lots of pictures for myself of the various countries I was in, of normal subjects, places, people and scenery that had nothing to do with the war. I had by now built up quite a big collection, especially of Egypt.

At G.H.Q. Middle East, we always worked in the mornings and evenings, having the afternoons off when not too busy, so that we could get exercise out of doors in daylight. I was out almost every afternoon when in Cairo, down in the Mousky, into the Citadel and some of the famous mosques, in the squares and streets, and even into the surrounding countryside. Cairo buildings stopped abruptly not very far from the centre, where the fields of the Nile Delta began, so it was easy to just walk out into the country. I used to take a tram to certain spots and then leave the city behind and immerse myself in the lush green of the crops.

Hardly any Europeans ever did this, even in peace time; I was told it was dangerous. But I did find an occasional companion among the forces, especially an army doctor who loved the countryside as much as I did. The peasants were always friendly, wherever I went in Egypt. Here and in other parts of the country I often wandered through the villages, taking photographs and trying to talk to the people. Sometimes I was invited into the houses for sweet tea, occasionally even for meals. It was only after I returned to England that I discovered that all villages in Egypt were out of bounds to troops. A fine soldier I was!

My original Ilford film ran out after a time. Then I used captured Agfa film brought in from the desert and when that supply dried up I was able to use short ends from our cine department, loading them into my own cassettes. I was thus never out of 35 mm film, but developers were harder to get. I had to do a lot of experimenting and trying unknown developers. But I was able to build up a collection of thousands of negatives of the Middle East, a wonderful asset after I returned home.

Then one day a cable arrived from the War Office: 'Return Cash to London immediately, by air if possible.' I wondered what new job they had for me and started to pack. Many things had to go by sea, with a good chance of them being lost on the way. But one item that went with me, at the expense of anything else, was my precious collection of negatives. They, in their albums, and my camera, took up about half my allotted baggage allowance but I did not mind. We took off at midnight a day or two later and flew to Gibraltar. Then on another midnight we took off for an airport in Cornwall. First we flew well out into the Atlantic before we turned northwards because the enemy still occupied France and we did not want to be shot down over the Bay of Biscay.

At daybreak we found we were approaching south-west Ireland, having been blown far off course, and our Polish pilot was completely lost. For hours we flew all over Ireland, then at last across the Irish Sea to land in Cornwall after mid-day, having by then been posted missing. We were cold, tired and very hungry, after flying all that time in an unheated bomber. But we were welcomed most warmly at the R.A.F. station, given lashings of drink and an excellent lunch. In the evening we were put on a train for London.

The phone at the airport was out of action so I had not been able to phone Betty to tell her I was home. She had been tipped off by the War Office that I would be coming home soon but did not know just when. I could only phone her next morning from Paddington Station, then take a taxi and go home. It was quite a reunion. All this long time apart seemed to make no difference at all. We just took up our old life again immediately, as if we had never been separated at all. She was by now managing a large block of flats in Chelsea and so had not joined any of the women's forces. It was grand to be home again, but what now?

I went down to the War Office. I had heard in Cairo that they might want me to go out to India, perhaps to head the Army Film and Photo Unit under Admiral Mountbatten. This turned out to be the case. I declined the offer with thanks; I had had enough of hot climates. I was on a civilian contract and could please myself. So we parted company, but most amicably. I came away with a certificate of good conduct and a month's leave. I signed on at the Appointments Branch of the Ministry of Labour where I was told that I had better find a job that appealed to me or they would have to give me the first suitable photographic job that came along, even darkroom work. I had a month to do something about it.

CHAPTER SIX

The British Council

In the Middle East, towards the end of my career there, I had been asked to do a lot of lecturing for the British Council, on the work of our unit. G.H.Q. had been pleased about this and gave me time off to do it. I travelled about over much of Egypt, to various towns, and even went up to Jerusalem to lecture there. When I was leaving Cairo, the British Council insisted on giving me a letter of introduction to their headquarters in London. Now was the time to use it.

I had an offer to become features photographer for one of the national newspapers—they were very eager to have me—but the Ministry of Labour decreed that this was not an essential job. I must try to find something more important. I went round to the British Council, found they needed another photographer and I got the job. This was approved by the Ministry and I settled down to two years of most enjoyable work, with delightful companions and a feeling that I was doing something really worth while. The other photographer was Harold White, who had made a name for himself for superb industrial photography, using a Rolleiflex, with his own technique of flash lighting. He and I became good friends from the moment we met and have remained so ever since. I learnt a lot from Harold who eventually weaned me from exclusive 35 mm photography on to the Rolleiflex. I still use 35 mm, with a Pentax now, but only as an extra camera for special jobs.

The purpose of the British Council was to publicize Britain abroad, to tell the rest of the world about the British way of life. The Ministry of Information did the day to day stuff; the British Council did the more sophisticated cultural side, in the broadest sense, taking in science, literature, music, theatre, medicine, industry, local government, transport and so on. I soon saw that the photographic department, under Leonard Forsdick, was very well run. Everyone, from photographer to darkroom assistant, took a pride in the job, anxious only to produce prints of the highest quality. Projects were done thoroughly, with time in hand so that they could be finished properly, even allowing for weather, and there was always time between jobs to finish developing films and doing the captions. A new project was only started when the previous one was finished. To me, this is the right way to do photography, but how rarely can it be achieved.

Photographs were widely used by the British Council, which was a semi-official body under the aegis of the Foreign Office. Each department, staffed by experts, had a pleasing degree of independence within a general framework and carried out its own projects. We illustrated many of these projects with our photographs, and we initiated many ideas ourselves. Pictures were sent out to many parts of the world, particularly after the war was over, often made up into big sets for display purposes, with smaller prints for publication. Our department, even when I joined the Council, was turning out over 300,000 prints each year. Soon, many of mine were among them.

I carried out many different assignments for the Council. The first one was on gold beating, one of the real old crafts still in existence. Then I did a big project in a Lancashire cotton mill, showing every process from the raw cotton to the finished cloth. This was right up my street, similar to work I had done on my own before the war. Another story followed in the north, on the Manchester Ship Canal, something that appealed to me very much as I had lived near the banks of this Canal up in Cheshire as a school boy and been greatly interested in the ships that found their way from the Mersey estuary to the heart of Lancashire.

While I was with the Council, we built up big photographic stories on typical towns and villages. Harold did Leicester as an industrial city, and Laycock as an old English village. I did Richmond, Yorkshire, as an English market town. I went up there and stayed for two weeks, photographing every aspect of that lovely old town and the surrounding countryside, farms, horse studs, dairies, the market and all the activities of the people. I photographed a meeting of the town council and later on the mayor at work in his shop. Troops in the barracks and the local fishing society on the River Swale all came into focus. It was a pleasant assignment and I got to know everyone in Richmond. Months later, we put on a big exhibition of my photographs in the town, so that the people of Richmond could see what I had made of it.

The war finished not so long after I joined the Council, and we then proceeded to do a big story on Ulster, where nothing had so far been done by the Council. Harold and I went over for a whole month and between us we covered Belfast, Londonderry and other towns, many industries, shipping, farming, local government and we were also highly privileged to photograph Parliament in session. This was, we believe, the first time that parliament anywhere in the British Empire had been photographed actually in session.

We worked out everything with the Clerk of Parliament, and between us we covered every aspect of parliamentary life. We were allowed to use flash in the House, as long as we did not cross the bar. To our great delight, Parliament was suddenly prorogued while we were there and we photographed all the pomp and ceremony that goes with that. It took some working out but by rushing around a bit we missed nothing of this important aspect of the parliamentary system. A month or so later we returned to Belfast to cover the opening of the new Parliament, so in the end we really did get everything.

Those pictures went literally all over the world and were used for many years afterwards. We put on a big exhibition of our photographs in Belfast which was opened by the Prime Minister of Northern Ireland, Sir Basil Brooke, a man we had got to know quite well during our work. It created a lot of interest.

During my period with the British Council I was allowed to develop my freelance work in my own time. Betty had kept a few embers glowing while I was abroad and I quickly opened up some markets again. I began selling my Middle East pictures in a quite satisfactory way. This was when I wrote my first book, *Living on my Camera* (*Focal Press*), and I also wrote many articles as well.

During my second year with the Council I took the full six weeks holiday to which I was entitled, all at the same time, so that Betty and I could go to Sweden. We were to be the guests of the Swedish Tourist Organization and the Swedish Foreign Office. This was arranged through a friend of ours who was doing public relations work for Sweden and who knew of our potentialities as journalists, having seen much of what we had done.

We were treated royally in Sweden and saw much of that beautiful Scandinavian country. We particularly fell in love with the Swedish west coast, with its thousands of islands and its wide scattering of the most colourful fishing villages. We photographed scenery, people, cities, towns, villages, festivals, steelworks, power stations, docks and shipping and even women's fashions in one of the big shops. We managed to get enough motoring pictures to be able to write an article after our return home on motoring in Sweden. Even more important, we had a long illustrated article accepted by the *Queen* on 'Sweden Today', a real joint effort where Betty wrote the article herself and I supplied the pictures. It was a most valuable return to foreign travel.

In my second year with the Council I earned as much again as my salary from freelance work. It was all building up to the time when I should return to freelance work entirely. Nice though it was to work for the Council, the urge to be on my own again began to assert itself. I emerged from the direction of labour controls, after the war was over, and could start on my own whenever I wanted to. The decision was made for me when, rather suddenly, the powers-that-be decided that the British Council should not operate a photographic department of its own but should have all its photographic work done by the Central Office of Information.

To all of us, this was a disastrous decision. The C.O.I., with all respect to them, had very different ideas of how photography should be done. Gone was our idea of the team spirit, we thought, the pride in the job—all the things we valued most highly. Most of the unit went over to the C.O.I. I didn't. This was just the kick in the pants that I needed. I left and started on my own again. Harold White stuck it for a year and then left in utter disgust. He could not stand it any more. He became a highly successful freelance industrial photographer and made a great name for himself.

I am a great believer in good luck, though I would never really count on it. Some people are just plain unlucky, others get a break time after time, without any effort on their part. I feel that I have had almost more than my share of good luck at times throughout my career. I had one such break when I started to freelance again. Accommodation was very difficult to get after the war; vacant darkrooms ready for use were unheard of. Yet I found one, right away. A friend at the Camera Club, where Harold and I were both members, told me of an advertizing friend of his who, he believed, had a darkroom to let. I went right round to see him, found he knew of me and he had, indeed, got a nice little darkroom in a small office building in Grays Inn Road for which he wanted a tenant. I took it immediately, at quite a modest rent. I was set up.

And so this brings me to the end of my first book and a little way beyond, to the point where I started out once again as a freelance and began to build my business up to where it is today. So if you read my original book years ago, and have skipped these pages up to here, this is where you begin again, where I describe my experiences and travels after the end of the war and how Betty and I have worked as a team. Whether it is as good a story as the first part, you must be the judge.

CHAPTER SEVEN

Freelancing Again

Long ago, when I was trying hard to become a writer and a good photographer, in my spare time in Canada, before I had plucked up enough courage to leave the security of my radio job, I used to day-dream of what I could do if I made a success of photo-journalism. Don't we all do this sort of dreaming at times? I could never really bring myself to believe that I would ever be able to travel anywhere I wanted, that I could go off to far-away parts of the world and stay for weeks or months on end. I must have thought I could make some sort of success of it, or I would not even have given it a try. As it turned out, my wildest dreams have come true. I have done more than I ever believed possible, since those days when I was working for the British Council in the immediate post-war years.

I have travelled through a hundred countries, been round the world, over the North Pole, round Africa by sea, across the Andes and the Rockies and into the Himalayas, to India by road, through the jungles of West Africa and I was one of the first photographers to be allowed into Red China with my cameras. I have travelled by road and rail, sea and air, on bicycle, horse-back, elephants and camels, on bamboo rafts and in dug-out canoes and on foot. I have travelled like this for many years now, but I still get a thrill at the prospect of more travelling.

I never tire of travelling itself. I may be exhausted at the end of a hard day's work but a good night's sleep will always put me right again. I get far more tired with all the work I have to do in London at the end of a trip, sorting out thousands of new photographs, identifying them and putting them in order. But that is all part of the job. I come back from every trip feeling that I have had a holiday, however hard I have been working. A holiday with nothing to do but lie in the sun would bore me to tears in no time. I like to travel with a purpose.

Soon after the end of the war, while I was still with the British Council, my wife left her war-time job, and we joined forces. I taught her to use a camera, a Rolleiflex, and soon discovered to my great joy that she possessed the one most important qualification—the seeing eye. She knew almost instinctively what made a good picture. Anyone can be taught to handle a camera properly and to produce a technically good photograph. But in the end it is what you photograph that matters, not how you do it. Betty has produced many masterpieces and been hung in the London Salon of Photography a number of times. Sometimes, when a specially good picture turns up, we fight over it, each claiming it as our own. Quite

44

often it turns out to be one of hers and this always pleases me. Together we have roamed the world as a team, each taking photographs, often going our separate ways for a few hours or days, occasionally even weeks, but always coming together again to pool our pictures and to write joint articles on our travels.

Now how is this done? We could not possibly make a go of this kind of work if we had to pay all our own expenses. So we often travel free, or for the most part free. But again, how is that done? Well, air lines, shipping lines, hotels and national tourist organizations all over the world welcome publicity, especially travel articles published in magazines and newspapers. Many of them reckon that an article on their particular air line, hotel or country, as the case may be, is worth at least ten times the same amount of space taken up in an advertisement. So they are prepared to give concessions to anyone who can get articles published. We do get articles published, so we receive invitations and concessions. It is as simple as that.

Simple, yes, once one is well established and can virtually promise that one really can get articles published. Not so simple when one is a beginner, with few if any established markets for articles. That is the time when one most needs help in the way of invitations, when one is probably broke or nearly so, working on a shoestring. Later on, when one is known and established, concessions are not quite so essential, though always welcome.

After I left the British Council we started, inevitably, in a small way for the first year or two. Our extensive foreign travels did not really start until the 1950's. We did a few trips in the British Isles, mostly at our own expense, to Lundy Island, The Wye Valley, Norfolk and Scotland, taking masses of photographs and later writing articles, a few of which were published. We went to Lundy twice, the first time because I suddenly received a request from the *National Geographic Magazine* (U.S.A.) to go over to the island to take a lot of photographs for an article they had on hand. The second time was for our own library.

The article in the *Geographic Magazine* was written by Colonel P. T. Etherton, a most interesting character, who came with us on both occasions to Lundy. He was the man who organized the flight over and round Mount Everest in 1933, a man whose whole life had been a series of adventures. We became good friends and often met together, at his home or ours. He liked Betty's cooking! With my pictures I was able, later on, to illustrate Colonel Etherton's book on Lundy—*Tempestuous Isle,* published by Butterworth Press in 1950.

In Scotland, on two different trips, we took a lot more pictures for the *National Geographic Magazine,* and these assignments helped considerably with our expenses in those early days. It would have been nice to continue doing work for this illustrious magazine but, more and more as the years went by, they tended to do almost all their own photography. They did, however, call upon me to help out at the Coronation in 1953, when virtually all their photographers were concentrated in London, under the leadership of Kip Ross. I took pictures of the ox-roast on Wimbledon Common for them. Most of their photographers that day were able to photograph only one subject, being allocated to one position and unable to move around. Two of my pictures were eventually published in the magazine and I was well recompensed.

I went out after a lot of industrial photography in those early days, and kept this up for many years, at home and abroad. I did several jobs for Taylor Woodrow, the big constructional people. They were operating an open-cast coalmine in South Wales and I went there during an appalling period of wintry weather, when the site was smothered in snow. But I still got some pictures. Other work for this firm included factories and power stations under construction, and years later a pre-fabricated housing factory in East Anglia.

I began a series of commissions for the London Brick Company. They wanted new pictures but did not know quite what they wanted. They left me alone to wander wherever I liked all over their vast clay pits and brick works in Bedfordshire, seeking good subjects and trying to dramatize them. It was fascinating work and I thoroughly enjoyed it.

The International Wool Secretariat got me to do some work for them in various mills in the north, as a result of my pre-war photography in the Cotswold mills that made billiard cloth. I did a big job in a tyre-retreading factory in Basingstoke. This took a bit of ingenuity because so much of the product and the surroundings were black in colour. I had to make use of flash lights in considerable numbers. The quick time exposure technique was not so easy to apply.

I spent one happy week going all over the various docks in South Wales taking pictures for the Great Western Railway Company. Ships always fascinate me, though in the course of my travels I must confess that much of the glamour of railways has rubbed off and disappeared. I also took a whole series of pictures for the Great Western of typical workers—a shunter, a guard, a driver, a porter, crane-driver, etc. more or less dramatic pictures of the men at work, a most interesting project.

I was commissioned by a firm near Brighton who made medicinal pills and tablets to take a number of photographs of their machines and processes, and this led to other work from time to time in their factory. I did a lot of work in several radio and battery works, and in a big paper mill in Derbyshire.

In all this indoor photography I used a combination of quick time exposures, either in existing light or in my own floodlights, and sometimes flash lights. Here I nearly always used two flashes, one on the camera, the other on an extension, in order to introduce some modelling and to avoid harsh shadows. I came to use floodlights less and less, as they were a lot of trouble, not only in setting them up but so often in blowing fuses and putting parts of the factory out of use. I tried at all costs not to be a nuisance to my clients, having heard lurid tales of other industrial photographers who sometimes nearly put them out of business with their massive lights.

I was asked to take a series of craftsmen for the Monsanto Chemical Company. These had to be real character studies of the men at work. In most cases I used the two-flash technique, taking several different shots of each subject. These included a tyre maker, a farmer holding a lamb, a teazle setter in a woollen mill, and so on. I won a silver cup at the Camera Club for my study of the tyre maker later on.

I secured another commission to do all the photographic work, some in colour, for an anniversary prestige book put out by a well known printing company. Subjects ranged all the way from huge printing presses to craftsmen binding books. Quite a challenge.

Another job was for a firm making poultry foods. They wanted to show their birds thriving on the special foods they produced, and here I ran into an un- expected trouble. In a big building housing hundreds of splendid looking hens, I had to use flash. The effect was incredible. As the flash went off every bird shot into the air as though jet-propelled and I was smothered with flapping wings and feathers and deafened by the most appalling screams from the panic-stricken birds. But the picture came out alright, though I could not use flash again.

One day a lady by the name of Gwen Cash wrote to me from Canada to see if we were related, but we could trace no common ancestors. Her family had been deeply involved in the needle industry in Redditch and she wanted to write a book all about it. Up till then it was still very much of a craft industry, carried out in small workshops. She came to see us and asked me if I would take a lot of photographs to illustrate her book. This was just the excuse I needed to tackle another industry, and I went up to the Midlands to do quite a big story on needles. The book never materialized but I made good use of the pictures in other ways.

I was asked to do several industrial jobs for a magazine called *Future,* an English magazine something like *Fortune* in America. It was most beautifully produced though, alas, it did not survive many years. They wanted colour photographs only, of such industries as aluminium rolling and fabrication, the then newly-opened Margam steelworks in South Wales, a cable works near Liver- pool where my instructions were to make copper look like copper and not something of a different colour. I also took a lot of photographs for them of the Glasgow docks.

Colour work in industry was not so highly developed in those days and lighting was always a problem. I confess now that I took many chances and got away with them, but at the same time I learnt a great deal. Most of the lighting was ar- tificial, though often mixed, so I generally used film for artificial light, taking a chance where some daylight came in through windows or sky-lights. Again, I used time exposures of various lengths as much as possible, the exact exposure being the critical feature. A certain amount of bracketing overcame this problem, though it was surprising how often all the pictures were usable. My pictures of aluminium really looked like that metal and not even like steel; my copper shone with a lovely warm glow, a pleasant surprise which I kept to myself. I secured some dramatic pictures of the furnaces and rolling mills at Margam, immediately after it opened. All this colour had to be done in 9 × 12 cm size, the only time I have gone outside roll film in all my photographic career.

I took a number of colour pictures for an advertising campaign for Standard Motors which used the title: 'All That's Best in Britain'. Subjects included a man fishing in the River Awe in Scotland, a close-up of a Beefeater in the Tower of London, Fulmer, a pretty village, and such like British subjects.

Another similar campaign was with Ferguson Tractors. I had to take many different pictures of these versatile machines being used in a wide variety of ways, in the Cotswolds and in the Lake District. I combined this with taking scenic and other pictures for my library, making a ten day trip in each of these beautiful districts.

One interesting proposal came my way, right outside my ordinary type of work, yet calling for some of the techniques I used in industrial photography. I was asked to illustrate a book entitled *How I Play Snooker,* by Joe Davis. He and I had several sessions together at a famous billiard hall when no one else was around. I had to photograph Joe adopting various stances, close-ups of his hands, his feet and so on. The pictures were to be as natural as possible, preserving the atmosphere of a billiard hall. Flash was therefore out because it would more or less black out the background, and it would create un-natural shadows over the table. I replaced the lights over the table with floodlight bulbs—the big ones of those days—and we got someone to stand by the main switch. We could not leave the lights on for more than half a minute or they would have started to melt in their own heat.

I used a fairly fast film and my Leica camera for all these pictures, many of them with a wide-angle lens but a few even with a telephoto lens, and every shot was a one second exposure at a small aperture. I worked on this technique until I had perfected it, then we got down to it. Joe was a delightful person to work with and we got on very well together. Forty-six of my pictures appeared in the book. A few years later I was asked to illustrate a second book by him called *Advanced Snooker.* I used the same technique and again achieved the results that were required. This time nearly a hundred pictures were used. Both books were published by Country Life Limited.

Not long after I had started on my own again, in that first year of 1947, I realized that I would not be able to do all the printing work myself, not if I was going to have time to travel and do industrial jobs and also give lectures. So I must face the question of employing a printer in my darkroom. The chief printer in the British Council darkrooms had been a lady known to one and all as 'Mack', actually Mary Mackmurdie, a real Londoner. She was just about the best printer I have ever come across—fast, clean and most conscientious, a rare combination these days. I had often talked to her in the darkrooms and I used to say:

'Mack, one of these days I shall go back to freelancing. Will you come and work for me then?'

I was really kidding but she took me seriously. So one day I phoned Mack and we met in a pub in Baker Street. She told me that she did not like working at the C.O.I. at all and would be glad to come and work for me. We agreed on a salary and she joined me soon afterwards. She was a bit lonely at first, as she was all alone in the darkroom, especially when I was away. But at least she was her own boss then and she stayed with me as a printer for twenty-two years. Then she retired at the age of sixty-five, but came in three days a week, not doing any prin-ting any more but all the other countless jobs that go with it.

She had managed all these, the numbering, sorting, spotting and trimming, as well as the printing—far more than the average printer will ever do, and she had the right sort of mentality to do the whole job swiftly and accurately. Soon she was bored with her days off and she came in full time, and as I write this she is still with us, a loyal and valuable worker if ever there was one.

With Mack as a printer, I got off to a good start. I never had to worry about the quality of the prints we turned out. Mack was her own severest critic and only the best was good enough for her. She was my severest critic, too, and always told me exactly what she thought of each new batch of negatives. I valued her opinion very highly and we always got along in an atmosphere of complete understanding. I don't think we have ever had a cross word in all the years we have been working together. Another example of my good luck.

I had one great stroke of luck in my first year that helped me to get on my feet rapidly. The Central Office of Information's photographic section was grossly overworked and it soon became apparent that it was quite incapable of doing the photographic work required by the British Council. So one day I received a phone call from Peggy Delius, a brilliant photographer herself, who was then in charge of the displays department of the Council. Would I be prepared to work for the Council on a freelance basis? I knew, of course, exactly the sort of photography that was required, as I had been doing it for the last two years. Naturally I said yes and promptly went round to discuss terms with Peggy, who had been with the Council longer than I had.

She wanted a lot of photography done, firstly on educational subjects, in schools, universities and technical colleges, and later on various other subjects. Great numbers of prints of different sizes would be required, some quite large, to be sent all over the world for display and publication, just the same as when I had been working in the Council. I agreed to a small fee for taking the pictures, knowing that I should make my money on the prints. The Council, of course, paid all my expenses for travelling, hotels and so on, when I was working exclusively for them.

After I had completed the first commission, in 1948, Peggy asked me to go to her office to discuss the prints she required. I came out almost reeling. The print order, which would be followed by more on the same subject, came to nearly £700. What a good job I had Mack in my darkroom! I always gave her a bonus when any of these big print orders was completed. There was quite a good profit on prints in those days, at standard rates, so that during the next two or three years I built up a handsome cash reserve as a sound foundation for my business.

During this period I did a number of jobs for the British Council, all over the country. When Betty and I went off on our own to Scotland and other parts, Peggy would get me to do a lot of 35 mm colour photography. These pictures were used to build up slides for lectures which were given abroad by British Coun-cil representatives in different countries. On one occasion some of my colour pictures of Scotland were shown to the Queen, now the Queen Mother, and I was told that she very much approved of them. The British Council work, with its big print orders, meant that I was never uncomfortably short of money after those early days. I don't mean that I made a quick fortune by any means, but I could take our travelling and office expenses, and the running of a car, in my stride without much worry. And it meant later, when we had to take on additional staff, that we did not have to think too hard before taking a chance. My work for the Council only terminated when the Treasury ruled against them employing outside photographers, and even then I supplied many prints from my negatives for quite a long time.Altogether, this was one of my luckiest breaks.

Before the war, as I have already explained, I had spent a long time in Bulgaria. I thought it would be interesting to go there again, so in 1948 I went to see the Bulgarian Minister in London. I told him of my pre-war trip to his country and showed him my articles and photographs that had been published. I said that I would like to go back again and see what they were doing under the new communist regime, and I would like to take Betty as well. A few months later, to my delight, approval was granted and we were given visas for a month's stay. We had to make our own way there, though, and this cost us £150 in air fares. But the Bulgarians put us up throughout our stay and took us all over their country. They were most generous and friendly and I met again some of the friends I had made there before the war.

We were invited to a big reception in the former Royal Palace in Sofia, given by the famous President Giorgi Dimitrov, now home in his own country again, of course. I had brought with me an enlarged and mounted print of one of the photographs I had taken of his mother before the war (she had died in the meantime), and I was able to present it to President Dimitrov at the reception. He seemed to be genuinely moved and most grateful.

The reception was in honour of the Hungarian premier, Rakosi, and other members of his Government. We were most amused to see the British Minister and his staff forcing themselves to look pleasant while they shook hands with the hated communist Hungarians. All very correctly done, of course, but it was obviously an effort on everyone's part.

I was able to revisit many of my favourite pre-war haunts in Bulgaria, and to take new photographs, including many this time in colour. I could still use a lot of my earlier pictures and in the next two years I succeeded in having various articles and picture features published on Bulgaria. It was a little-known country and I had a minor scoop, but it was a communist country now and not every editor was interested in it for that reason. However, I had a long illustrated article on Bulgaria as a whole in *Illustrated* the same year, and another one on Rila Monastery in *Picture Post*, both using colour pictures. I printed up my Fishing in Bulgaria pictures again and was happy to see them in a German magazine, and later in the Toronto Star. Pictures alone, in ones or small sets, continued to be published quite widely for some years. I made up a set on a priests' brigade working on a new road, a novelty but quite genuine. The English *Geographical Magazine* took a long article and pictures on Bulgaria and I had various other successes.

Apart from Bulgaria, I wrote numerous articles and made up various sets of pictures on other subjects into features. I did a lot of work with the English *Geographical Magazine* in those early days. Articles on the Midsummer Festival in Sweden, the Outer Hebrides, the Yeoman Warders of the Tower, Smögen—a Swedish fishing village, and a wood carver in Sweden all appeared within two years, as well as a series on British rivers—the Avon, the Wye and the Tyne. I went back to the Cotswolds and took some more pictures of billiard cloth being made, and then wrote an article for the *Geographical Magazine* all about it.

Betty, as I have said, had her first solo article published in 1946, in *The Queen*, on Sweden Today. Later, I had one in the same magazine on the Borromean Islands, after we had been to the Ticino region of Switzerland in 1949. *The Queen* remained a steady market for us for many years. Another woman's magazine where our articles appeared quite frequently was *The Lady,* starting with Dining out in Sweden, then the Ticino in Spring. *The Sphere,* now most regrettably defunct, took sets of pictures on a wide variety of subjects for many years, one of the first being on Hydro-electric Developments in Scotland and another on the island of Barra. It is a tragedy for freelance photographers that *Picture Post, Illustrated, The Sphere* and other picture magazines all went to the wall. Their demise restricted our markets and made the sale of picture features much more difficult.

One commission for *Illustrated* was to photograph the Houses of Parliament in colour four times during the same day, i.e. at 8 a.m., mid-day, 4 p.m. and sunset. I managed this literally all on the same day, in July 1947, and the editor published the pictures as a double-page spread. Another similar spread was on Springtime in Burnham Beeches, also in colour.

We supplied many sets of pictures to *Pictorial Education,* a splendid magazine with quite big pages. We got to know the editor, Hilda Cruise, very well and she liked us to suggest subjects to her where we could supply suitable pictures. Early successes with this magazine included the Roman Wall, Rose Oil in Bulgaria, Winter in Canada, Stratford on Avon, Lundy Island, Fishing in Sweden, Robert Louis Stevenson (I did this for the British Council as well while in Scotland), dates in Egypt, the Hungarian Puszta, Austria in Winter, Peat in Scotland, Harris Tweed, and Birds on the Farne Islands. Later, many more subjects were added to the list, until Miss Cruise retired, then the policy of the magazine was changed. It was nice to see our pictures reproduced so large, often 14 inches by 10.

During those early post-war years I became involved in books. *Living on my Camera* whetted my appetite for writing more books myself. Through a most valued introduction from W. A. Poucher, the famous mountain photographer, to Chapman and Hall, I interested them in doing a series, similar to his mountain books, on British rivers. I started on the River Avon, covering this gentle river from source to mouth. No one seemed to know just where it begun but I traced it up to Naseby, in Northants., and there I asked local people where was the actual source of the Avon. A bright school boy showed me a dried up artificial pool in a private garden, with a statue of a swan in the centre. The boy told me that, years ago, the source of the Avon was a spring which had been enticed to spout out from the swan's mouth and fill the pool. But now, he said, the source was in the cellar of a nearby pub. I went in to see the owner of the pub and he said: 'Yes, the Avon does indeed start in my cellar. Come, and I will show you.'

He took me downstairs and lifted up a flagstone in the cellar floor. Sure enough, a tiny spring bubbled up out of the ground but immediately disappeared down a small hole. He told me that it came up again in a field a hundred yards away. I went to see this second source, as it were, and thus I found the beginning of the River Avon.

It was most pleasant following the river all the way down to its mouth, at Tewkesbury, where it flowed into the Severn. Covering the whole river took several different trips, but eventually I made up a set of eighty pictures on all aspects of the river and the places through which it flowed, wrote some twenty thousand words both historical and personal, and the book was published under the title *Shakespeare's Avon*, in 1949. It was, I think, beautifully produced, with each of the pictures full page.

Before it saw the light of day I started on another river, the Wye, the one that starts on the slopes of Plynlimmon, in central Wales, and finishes below Chepstow on the Bristol Channel. This, I claimed, was the most beautiful river in Britain, with hardly a flaw in its entire length. So far, no one has challenged my claim. This again took several journeys, spaced over more than a year, and as before I wrote about twenty thousand words and the book appeared as *The River Wye*, in 1952.

I made money on both these books, though neither of them broke any records. I did far better with *Living on my Camera*, but that one caught the post-war boom in new books, whereas that boom was dying out when my river books appeared, and we did not do any more. But they would have been well worth doing even if I had made nothing on them at all. They enabled me to add a lot of new pictures of Britain to my library. I was endeavouring at that time to increase my library of pictures on the British Isles and this was a good way of doing it. The pictures were used in many other ways, and as already mentioned, helped to illustrate articles I wrote for the *Geographical Magazine* on both these rivers.

Around this time I also did a lot of work for Robert Hale Limited. I illustrated some of the books on British counties and regions that they were bringing out, under the general editorship of my old friend Brian Vesey-Fitzgerald. They required forty-nine pictures in each of their books. I would receive a list of subjects required, from the author, perhaps seventy-five or more, from which the final selection would be made. Only first book rights were required, so the pictures remained my copyright and, together with the hundreds of others which I took at the same time, again helped to swell my library. I received a fixed sum for each book, paid my own expenses and took a chance on the weather. I usually more than broke even but in any case these trips were a good investment. My British pictures grew to many thousands over a few years. The books appeared in the early 1950's. The counties I covered included Nottinghamshire and Northants., and the regions took in The Weald of Kent, The Fen Country, The Peak District and Galloway in Scotland.

For another publisher I did a similar thing on Suffolk, and Brian Vesey-Fitzgerald asked me to illustrate a book on Winchester which he wrote himself. In all these cases there were specific subjects required, sometimes small details, such as a corner of a building, or an ancient bridge. In the Fen Country I had to find one of the old fen farmers, almost the last of the originals, living far off any road in his little shack. I also had to find and photograph a famous iron stump in the midst of a wood, an almost impossible task. I came out of the wood torn and bleeding after scrambling to the site through masses of brambles. I enjoyed this work very much. It needed Ordnance Survey maps to find some of the subjects, almost like a treasure hunt.

My father often came with me on these trips. He was always a great country lover, active in all the preservation societies right up to his death at the age of eighty-five. My mother, unfortunately was bed-ridden for the last few years of her life, and they were both living in a nursing home. My father was almost too devoted to my mother and worried about her a lot. It was good for him to get out with me into the countryside he loved so much, and I found him a most interesting companion. He knew so much about birds and flowers and we were, I think, excellent companions on such trips. He was quite happy to go anywhere and he took a great interest in my work. In his younger days he had written the nature notes for the *Manchester Evening News* for more than thirty years, and many other articles, and had had two books published on the British countryside.

In 1948 Fountain Press asked me to write a book on Leica Photography, a project I greatly enjoyed. They produced a most handsome volume, with a number of pictures, a few in colour, and it sold well, running into new editions, suitably revised, in 1952 and 1955. Another book I did for Fountain Press came about as a result of an article of mine which appeared in *Photography,* on the subject of a boy's first camera. I used my small nephew to show what could be done with a cheap camera, making all the mistakes possible and learning from them. Fountain Press suggested a book—Boy's Book of Photography. This saw the light of day in 1953 and was republished in 1956. It went well, especially around Christmas time, and it made a good present for boys, and I really made money on this one.

About the same time, Hutchinsons commissioned me to write a book to go into a series they were producing on the theme '— on a Small Income'. Mine was, of course, on photography. It came out as a paper back, on which I received two old pence per copy, but quarter of the print was hard-backed, on which I received six pence per copy. As it ran into tens of thousands I found this was a most remunerative book.

Later on, in 1966, I was asked to bring it up to date and add colour, and it was reissued as an Arrow book, again selling in large numbers. Hutchinsons issued about thirty titles in the original form and in 1957 another one of mine appeared on 'Travel on a Small Income'. This meant a lot of work, as I had to check my information and writing with the tourist offices of every country in Europe, to be sure to get my facts right. But again, it was a big success and I continued to receive royalties from both these books for some years.

I never regard books as a regular source of income. I write them, they are published and I forget about them. Every six months I suddenly receive a statement of sales and a cheque and it always seems like a pleasant surprise, something I had not counted upon.

Over the years I wrote articles steadily for the various photographic magazines, for *Amateur Photographer, Miniature Camera Magazine, The British Journal of Photography, Photography* and others. I built up a very pleasant relationship with A. L. M. Sowerby, Percy Harris, Harold Lewis, Arthur Dalladay, to mention only a few, and with Reggie Mason who took over the editorship of *Amateur Photographer* when Sowerby retired. Writing has always been an important part of my work, and never more so than in those early days. Thank goodness I was born with some writing ability in me – I was never trained to write – otherwise my career as a photographer would have been considerably handicapped. Writing and photography make a powerful combination together.

These articles, and others in non-photographic magazines, together with the lecturing I did, and of course the various books in which I became involved, all helped to make my name known in those early days, in photographic and journalistic circles. And as important as anything else was a by-line under my photographs, where they were used alone, without my own writing. To this day I value these by-lines very greatly; they are a vitally important form of publicity, and as in most forms of business, publicity is essential. People, especially those who buy photographs for publication purposes, remember names under pictures and make at least a mental note of them for future reference.

I mention these various successes to show what I did with the many pictures I was gradually building up into a library. It is no use having lots of pictures if you don't do something with them. By using them myself, and writing articles around them, I gradually became known as a source of photographs. In time editors, publishers and other users of photographs began to get in touch with me to see if I had the particular subjects they required. Most times I did not, but as the years rolled by I could say yes more and more often. It was all a challenge to go on and on, taking more and more pictures, to cover the world, in fact.

This, by the way, is a total impossibility for any one person, in any one lifetime, but it has been a lot of fun trying. Today, the library runs itself, the demands for photographs being so many and so frequent that it takes my library staff of four girls all their time to keep up with them. What I have to do is to go on taking more and more pictures, trying to keep the library up to date and always adding new material. But this is jumping ahead quite a long time, so let us go back some years.

1 Bulgarian Harvest 2 The Moscow Circus

5 Gnu, Amboseli Game Reserve, Kenya   6 Lion in Lake Manyara National Park, Tanzania

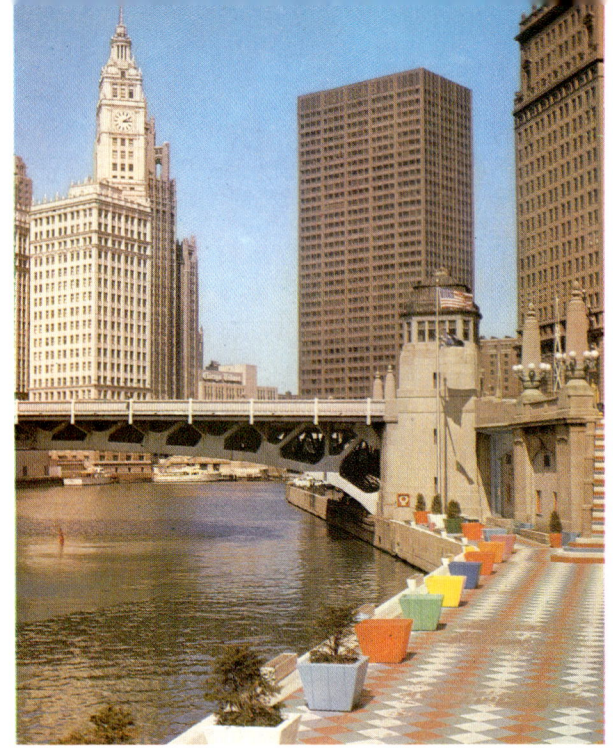

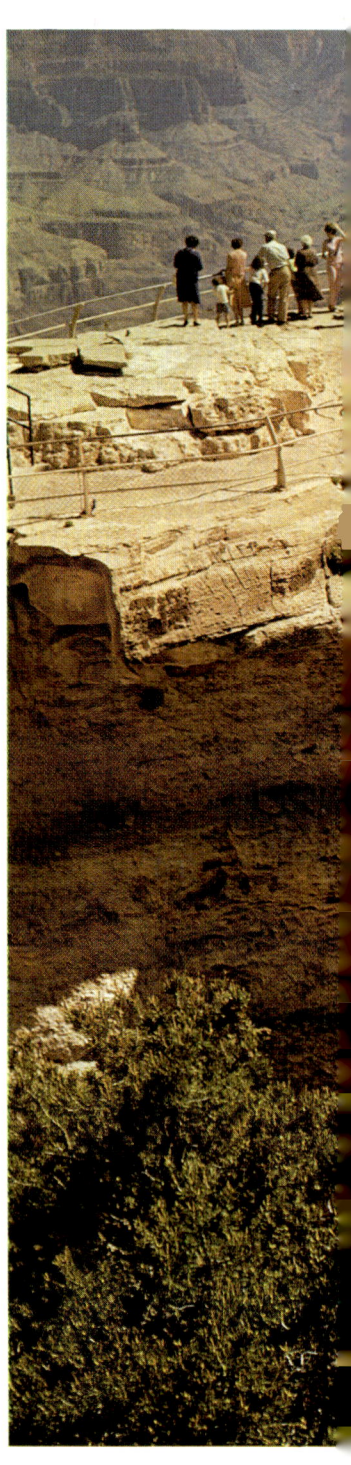

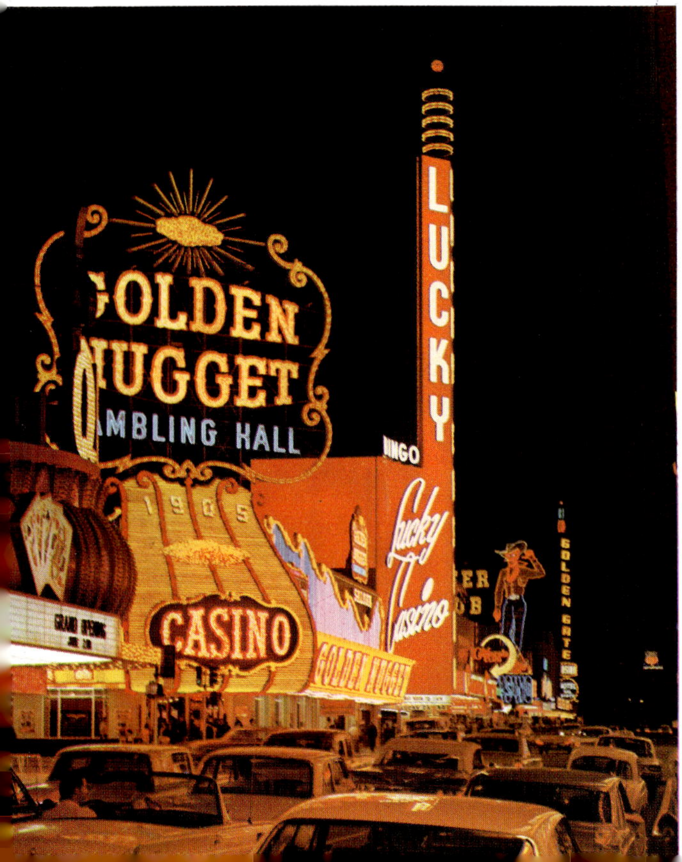
OLDEN
UGGET
AMBLING HALL
LUCKY
BINGO
1905
Lucky Casino
CASINO
GOLDEN NUGGET
GOLDEN GATE

10 A boy of the Ndebele tribe, South Africa
11 A peasant in Nepal
12 A miner off duty in South Africa

13 A wandering minstrel in Nepal 14 Indian woman carrying water near Delhi

15 Temple at Kelaniya, Ceylon
16 Pilgrims on the Ghats at Benares, India

17 Buddha at Kamakura, Japan

19 Mount Fuji from Izu Peninsula, Japan

18 Television studio at Riyadh, Saudi Arabia

20 Ghost gum in the Outback, Australia

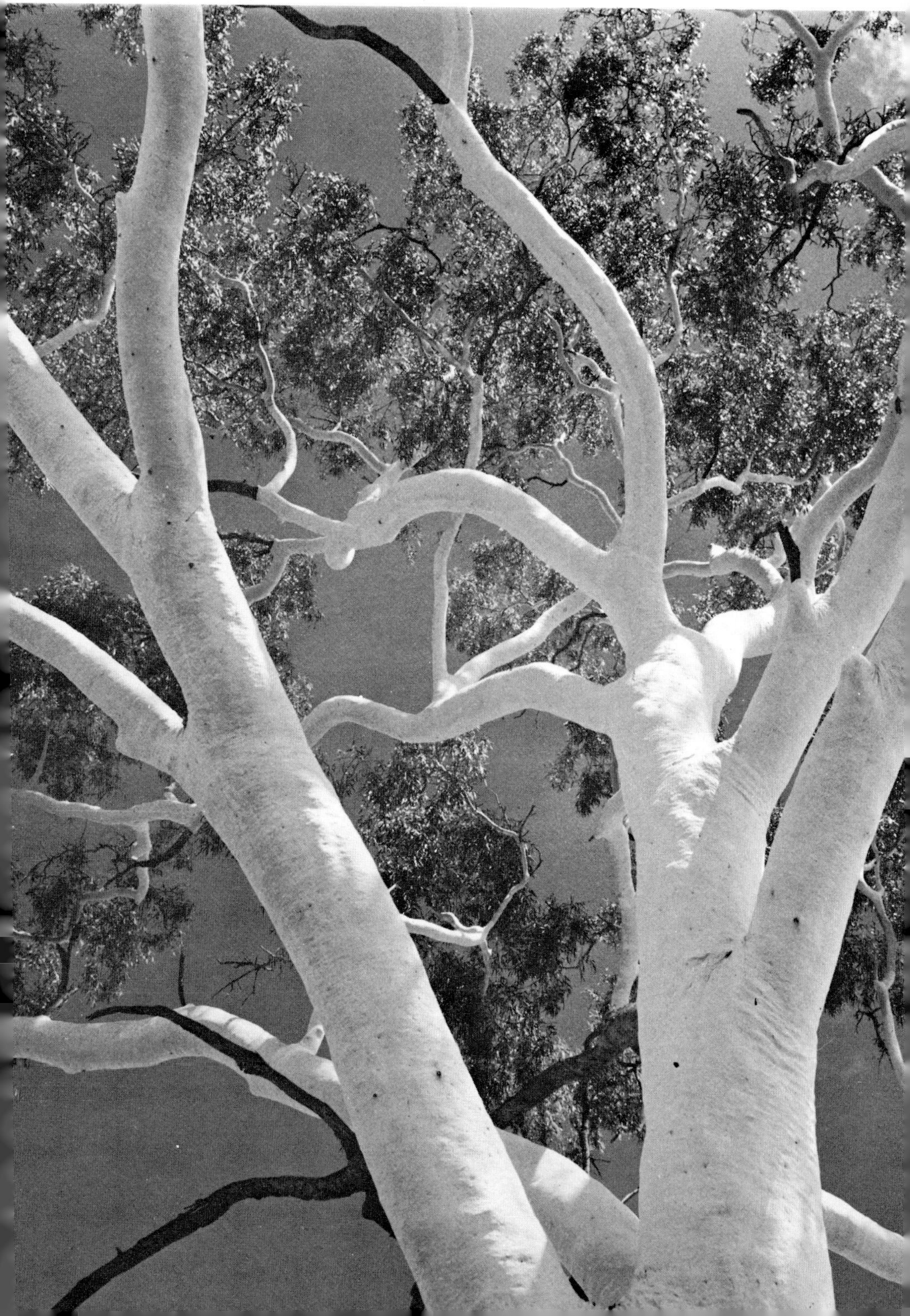

23 Steel workers at the Wuhan Steel Works, China   24 Demonstrators dispersing, Peking

Commissioned Trips

An essential part of the work of a freelance consists of making and maintaining contact with potential clients, going to see them, phoning or writing to tell them about new material recently added to the library, perhaps suggesting subjects for articles, and so on. Similarly, when travelling is such an important part of one's work as it is with us, it is equally essential to contact travel organizations who might be encouraged to grant us facilities to travel. Armed with a selection of our published material, and some samples of our photographs to show what we could do in the way of quality, we began to penetrate into the offices of publicity managers of shipping lines, air lines and the tourist offices of foreign countries.

We were not begging but offering a service to these people, suggesting that we could work together to our mutual advantage. Some of them knew us already, having seen our published articles and pictures. Which goes to show how important a by-line is under a photograph, whenever one can get it. Gradually we became known. We received invitations to promotional parties where we met other people, and we became known in the travel world, and one thing led to another. It still does. We go to many of these parties now, and gather much useful information from them. But we also go because we meet other people there and make useful contacts. Many of our trips have started from a cocktail party, or a luncheon given by some other country, or some travel agency.

Many of the people we met in those early days took us very much on trust. Publicity people often do this, judging for themselves whether a prospective writer is really worth gambling on. Inevitably, there are people who try to horn in on this sort of thing, promising the earth without the slightest chance of ever being able to do anything useful at all. Anything for a free trip! This does a lot of harm to genuine writers and photographers, making it all the harder to convince publicity officers that you are bona fide.

When someone gives you a concession he expects value for money. It always costs him something, often quite a lot, which comes out of his publicity budget. At the end of the year he has to account for the money he has spent. If he has provided trips to half a dozen journalists and has had no articles published as a result, he will be in serious trouble with his employers. So, if one wants to be a success at this type of work, one must be in a position to reciprocate fully. We have sometimes turned down an invitation because we did not think that we could honestly do anything worth while in return. Quite often, on the other hand, we have asked for a concession because we were sure we could give value.

We have done pretty well in this way for a number of countries over the years, and they are very pleased with us. After early beginnings we have proved that we really can get a lot of articles published, hence we are often asked back again. We almost regard Switzerland, for instance, as our second home, having been there so often, both in summer and winter. Norway is another country where we feel very much at home, and where we have been invited back time after time, and the same with Italy, to mention only three. Being freelances, we can often get several articles published, on any one country, in a variety of magazines and newspapers over a period of time.

We often write about a place or country for several years after we have been there. We think up likely markets and produce another article for them, probably slanted to their particular requirements. Sometimes we are specially asked to write an article on a certain country by an editor who knows we have been there. Our photographs also provide publicity for that country, whether they are published in magazines, books or newspapers, though this is not quite such valuable publicity as an article.

There are variations on this theme. Sometimes we are asked to visit a country or a town to take photographs specially for their own publicity purposes. In other words, we are commissioned to take photographs and we are paid for doing so. I always suggest in this case that we could do the work much cheaper if, at the same time, we could take photographs for our own library. No one to date has ever turned down this suggestion, because it holds so many advantages. Firstly, we reduce our fee substantially. Secondly, pictures put into our own library provide potential publicity for the town or country over a long period of time, and then, of course, we are most likely to be able to write articles as well after our return home. A bonus, as it were, which costs no one anything.

Several instances come to mind where we have made this arrangement—Malta, more than once; one of the Bahama islands; Nigeria, in West Africa; and the spa of Baden-Baden. In each case we have enriched our own library while carrying out the work for which we were commissioned, and everyone has been satisfied. It is one of the ways in which we are constantly adding to our library.

Sometimes a country or travel organization will ask us for some photographs in return for their invitation. Smaller countries in particular often run on a limited budget for travel publicity and so we agree to this plan. It is a simple matter to take some extra pictures to give to our hosts later. We try to make sure that these will not be handed out free in such a way that they might interfere with our own markets. But sometimes this does occur, so we are rather careful in making such an arrangement. Usually it works out very well and everyone is pleased with the results.

We have made this arrangement with various shipping and air lines, and have never regretted it. The first time we did this on a big scale was with the Union Castle Line, in 1952. They used to run a passenger service right round Africa years ago, going south through the Mediterranean, the Suez Canal and all the way down the east coast of Africa to Capetown, returning northwards through the Atlantic, or vice versa. The ships stopped at about twenty different ports, in a dozen countries, and it seemed to me that this would be a photographer's paradise. Especially as, up to then, we had done nothing on Africa, apart from my war-time Egyptian pictures.

I was completely unknown to Mr. Robson, the Union Castle publicity officer, when I bearded him in his office in the city. I showed him some of our cuttings and asked him if he would consider the idea of our travelling round Africa on one of their ships, in return for the publicity we could get for his line. I also offered to take some pictures for his own publicity purposes at the same time. He was interested and took my offer seriously. He doubted if his directors would agree to a free trip but thought they might give us a substantial reduction in fares. Mentally, I decided that this would not do but I said nothing. A few days later Mr. Robson phoned me to say that the directors had agreed to my suggestion and were prepared to give us a free trip all the way round Africa.

He suggested that we should go on the maiden voyage of the KENYA CASTLE and we agreed on the number of pictures we would take for them. We fixed a price for colour and black-and-white pictures and then worked out how many pictures at these prices would make up the value of our tickets. He also hoped we would be able to get some articles published that would bring them some good publicity. It seemed to be a good arrangement all round. Union Castle took us at face value and hoped for the best. We hoped to get a mass of new photographs for our library to justify the ten weeks that the trip would take. As it happened, it was a bigger success for both of us than we had ever anticipated.

We were blessed with good weather everywhere and we came back with far more pictures than we had expected. We gave Union Castle first choice and they seemed to be very pleased. Of course, it is not merely a matter of supplying an agreed number of photographs. Any amateur could do that. The pictures must be the right kind for publicity purposes, with suitable subjects taken in good lighting, imaginative pictures, not just dull hackneyed subjects. Colour must usually be on 120 size, not 35 mm. Above all, the pictures must be technically good, outstanding wherever possible. We did our best wherever we went.

We were able to get several articles published soon after our return and have had many others since. Ilford Limited, whose films we used for all black-and-white pictures, offered to put on a big exhibition of our pictures at their Holborn Galleries. They approached Union Castle for co-operation and this was readily forthcoming, in the way of ship's models and other sea-going equipment which enhanced the exhibition considerably. In the end, the exhibition travelled all over the country, to all the main cities of the British Isles, during a period of two years.

Fountain Press suggested my writing a book on this voyage, copiously illustrated with our black-and-white and colour pictures. They co-operated with Union Castle and produced a most handsome volume which sold well on all the Union Castle ships for years afterwards.

All this publicity for Union Castle was indeed a bonus, very much appreciated, and one that I could not have foreseen before we set sail. Three years later Mr. Robson asked us if we would return to South Africa and take photographs for them of the interior and of Rhodesia, a proposition that we jumped at without hesitation. More of this later.

Air lines are not normally allowed to give free trips abroad to journalists without a definite commitment regarding publicity afterwards. This is a strictly enforced rule of the International Air Transport Association; an air line stepping out of line in this respect can be fined many thousands of pounds. We have made various arrangements with different air lines, sometimes guaranteeing to get articles published with a good mention for them within a year, sometimes agreeing to give them pictures up to the value of our tickets. These are known as barter deals and are entirely legal.

Another way to get over this problem is to pay for one's journey like a normal passenger and to send in an account for the same amount as soon as an article is published. This is done, of course, in agreement with the airline. It is not an arrangement I like and I have never made use of it myself. I feel that an airline should have more faith than that with a journalist who has proved himself over many years.

The only time that an airline is allowed to give a free ticket to a journalist is on an inaugural flight, i.e. the opening flight of a new service, or the introduction of a new type of aircraft on an existing service, when an airline wants to attract as much publicity as possible. Many times we have received invitations from British European Airways, T.A.P., the Portuguese Airline, Swissair, Quantas, Air Canada, K.L.M., the Dutch Airline, and others. We have made these the basis for trips to such countries as Belgium, Italy, Turkey, France, Portugal, Malta, Cyprus, Rhodes, Gibraltar, Switzerland, Tunisia, Ceylon, Canada and even Australia.

One of two things happens on an inaugural flight. The country concerned may take the opportunity of inviting the journalists on the flight to be their guests for a few days and to see something of the country while they are there, an economical way of securing publicity. The other alternative is that the journalists make their own arrangements with the country concerned and work out a stay to suit themselves. This, of course, depends on the country being convinced that it will be worth their while to put up a particular journalist up in hotels and transport him around the country. We have done both.

We have had some wonderful trips that were extremely useful where we went round with the other journalists on an inaugural flight, and we have on other occasions made special arrangements for ourselves. We can work fast with our cameras when we find ourselves in a good position to take photographs, and we think we can make the best of a given situation. But we can often do better and much more when we are on our own, partly because we can go at our own pace, stop where we like and within reason take as long as we like in any given place. It is annoying to other people in a party if you keep them waiting and if you want to keep jumping out of a car or coach to take photographs. When you are on your own it does not matter; you have only your guide to contend with and it is the guide's job to do everything possible to give you what you want.

I can see some of my readers getting hot under the collar, indignantly proclaiming that this is a racket.

'Give me a trip on your airline and I will praise it to the skies in my next article.'

'Put me up in your hotel for a few days and I will tell the world how wonderful it is.'

I can assure you that this is not the case at all. There may be a few unscrupulous publicity managers who will offer something in return for a guaranteed good mention, but I have never encountered one. No self-respecting journalist would agree to anything like this. We who are members of the Guild of Travel Writers are very particular about our freedom to write as we please. Under no circumstances will we be bound to write favourably about anything unless we honestly believe we are writing the truth. Our hosts, whoever they may be, have to take a chance on what we write. If they have a good product we will give it the praise we think it deserves. If we find faults that we think should not be there, we state the facts. We may never be asked back again but we never let this interfere with our judgement or our writing. It can be a salutary experience for the offending organization and often results in things being put right pretty quickly. This situation does not occur very often but we insist on our independence to write as we please.

So this, in brief, is how we work as freelance camera journalists, how we are able to travel about all over the world and what we have to do in return for the valuable concessions that are granted to us. But no one should imagine from my remarks that all our travelling is entirely free. Far from it. Despite the many concessions we get, some of our trips are quite expensive. In recent years, for instance, we have found that on what was an "everything found" invitation, the many extras that we have had to pay ourselves have come to nearly as much as a complete package tour to the same country, an indication of the extraordinary bargains that many package tours are today. But of course we often have the privilege of a car and a guide to ourselves, perhaps a better hotel room and first class travel, invitations to dine at special places, and so on, items which would not be included in a package tour. And we are sometimes asked to bear part of the cost ourselves, as will be seen in subsequent chapters.

Now let us look in more detail at some of the more interesting travel we have done, either together or myself alone, and see how it all worked out and what we made of it photographically.

CHAPTER NINE

Around Africa

Our trip around Africa in 1952 on the Union Castle ship KENYA CASTLE, already referred to, was an introduction not only to Africa, but also to parts of Europe, to the wild animals of Africa and of course to sea travel and cruising, an important part of the travel picture. It also gave us the first of the Napoleon Islands—St. Helena, and a brief look at the Canary Islands. Altogether a rich packet.

We were intrigued with Gibraltar and managed to explore much of that famous rock in the hours ashore. We have returned several times since, by sea and air, and seen it grow to a real holiday resort, not merely a stopping off place. Marseilles, our next port of call, has become a favourite of ours, especially all round the huge inner harbour, gay with fishing boats, ferries and private yachts. Genoa we found to be a large noisy city, none too clean, but the highlight here was a day out to Rapallo, Santa Margherita and best of all, Portofino. We had lunch there, sitting out in the open by the harbour. We completely fell for this delightful little port, its colourful buildings and long narrow harbour. It has certainly been highly developed and in the season it must be quite intolerable with all the day trippers, but out of season it is one of the places which makes me feel like a schoolboy, eager to go everywhere and photograph everything. We go back whenever we can.

Before leaving England, we were told that we probably would not be allowed ashore at Port Said, and certainly not allowed to take photographs. Relations between Britain and Egypt were somewhat strained at that time, though it was, of course, long before Suez or the Six Day War. Passengers on ships going through the Suez Canal were sometimes confined to their ships. But the Union Castle agents in Port Said had been informed of our presence on the KENYA CASTLE and had promised to do what they could for us.

The ship arrived quite early in the morning and tied up. As we were dressing in our cabin, we received a message that two police officers wished to see us. That settled it, we thought, and had visions of being locked in our cabin while the ship was in port. I went out to see them. They greeted me in a most friendly fashion and one of them said:

'Mr. Cash, we understand that you and your wife would like to take photographs of Port Said while your ship is in port. We would like to escort you and we have a launch waiting to take you round the harbour. Afterwards, we will take you into the town in a car.'

They were as good as their word. We were whisked away from the ship in a beautiful fast launch and they took us wherever we wanted to go. I took a picture of our ship in colour, with a lovely sky beyond, that was used for years afterwards by Union Castle as a large framed picture hung in travel offices. We saw it in various parts of the world in our subsequent travels.

Having covered the harbour and its shipping pretty well, we went ashore to meet the chief of the harbour police in his office, and were offered the traditional Turkish coffee. Then we jumped into a car and were driven into the town. Our fellow passengers, we discovered later, were allowed ashore but only to go to the big Simon Arzt shop near the ship. We went off into forbidden territory with our police escort, two young officers who spoke excellent English. I told them that I remembered Port Said from my war time days and that seemed to please them. Several times I asked them to stop while we got out to take photographs. Every request was granted. At one point a policeman on the street was so astonished to see me, an obvious foreigner, with a camera, that he came over in quite a menacing attitude, presumably to arrest me. But one of our escorts jumped out of the car and quickly pacified him.

We had been told that our ship would sail at 11 a.m. and all passengers must be aboard well before then. Eleven o'clock came and our guides showed no signs of returning to the harbour. I asked if it was not time for us to go back to our ship.

'Don't worry, Mr. Cash,' one of the officers replied. 'I am the traffic officer today and your ship cannot sail until I say so. We will go back soon.'

We did get back at 11.25 and were politely escorted up the gangway right on to the ship. Our fellow passengers, seeing us returning apparently under police guard, were quite sure that we had been arrested and were being forcibly returned to the ship. They were rather puzzled when they saw the effusive and most friendly way our police escort bade us farewell.

I always enjoy going through the Suez Canal. So much traffic went through this waterway between the Mediterranean and the Red Sea that for many years ships had been formed up into convoys, operated on strict schedules, with one-way traffic only, in alternate periods. Convoys were able to pass each other in the Great Bitter Lakes and in a loop of the canal built specially for this purpose. Incidentally, when Egypt seized the Suez Canal in 1956, it was thought that, with most of the foreign pilots dismissed, they would be unable to operate it themselves. On the contrary, their own pilots made an excellent job of it, getting all the ships through just as quickly and safely. Furthermore, in the following few years the canal was deepened by several feet, enabling bigger ships than ever to go through, especially the ever larger oil tankers.

Aden, except in the hottest part of the year, is a most interesting port. One of the driest places in the world, it rarely rains there, yet from a height we could see mountains to the north wreathed with heavy clouds where rain was falling and the country was quite green. I always remember that, when I was going out to Suez on the troopship during the war, a tremendous rainstorm hit Aden one night as we lay in the harbour, perhaps the first rain for several years. I was sleeping out on deck, fortunately under cover, but even so the spray from the rain almost drove me indoors.

But there was no rain on this occasion. We explored the whole town, including Crater, the old part, and we went far out into the surrounding desert, to the great salt pans and to the frontier at Sheikh Oman where we sat in an open café with the local Arabs sipping thick black coffee.

Our ship remained for a whole week at Mombasa and here many passengers left us. They were mostly people working and living in East Africa, returning from home leave. Many others joined us, going on leave and taking the opportunity of a long cruise around the Cape and home that way. One cynic said that many did this because they could not afford several months' stay in England and this was one way to use up some of the time. Nowadays everyone flies and so the problem does not arise in the same way. I don't know how true it was.

We went up by train overnight to Nairobi and stayed at the famous Stanley Hotel. The climate of Nairobi was delightful, fresh and cool, especially after dark, as it stands over five thousand feet above sea level. We were driven into the Nairobi National Park, a game sanctuary that starts only three miles from the city centre. It is remarkable place, and contains nearly all the well known African animals except elephant. It is fenced only along the railway line, to keep the animals off the rails. The other boundaries are wide open, so the animals may come and go as they please. They find it safer to remain within the park and they know the boundaries as well as any warden.

You can sometimes see the wild animals, including lions, with the buildings of the city on the sky line beyond. We saw virtually everything on this occasion except lion, which was a disappointment. Years later we made up for this. We flew to Nairobi, leaving our home at 4 p.m. and arriving in Nairobi at 9 a.m. the following morning. We went out to the game park the same day and saw five different prides of lions, all within less than twenty-four hours from leaving our home in London.

We also made a long motor trip down into the Rift Valley, on the splendid road built by Italian prisoners of war captured in Abyssinia (now Ethiopia) in the early stages of the Second World War. They had even built a little memorial chapel on a hillside, a beautiful piece of work. We went back to Mombasa in time to spend a week-end at the nearby Nyali Beach Hotel, bathing in the warm waters of the Indian Ocean, dancing in the moonlight out of doors after dinner.

As we left our ship on the Saturday morning to go to Nyali Beach, a little Indian shoemaker offered to make a pair of crocodile-skin shoes for Betty over the week-end. The price would be £3 and he swore they would be ready by the Monday morning. Otherwise, nothing to pay and the same if they were not a good fit. All he did was to draw the outline of her feet on a piece of paper. We did not expect to see him again. But when we returned to the ship after our week-end, the little man was squatting outside our cabin door, with the shoes in his hands. They were beautifully made and a perfect fit. Betty still has them and they have been greatly admired by well known shoe makers in this country.

We called at Zanzibar next, surely one of the most romantic-sounding places in the world. It came up to all our expectations. It is truly an island of scents, for it produces most of the world's cloves, along with its twin island Pemba, close by. The cloves are picked and laid out to dry in the sun, hence the perfume which can sometimes be detected far out to sea. It is a most luscious island, dense with greenery, dappled with the shadows of coconut palms which cover nearly all the land. We wandered all through the narrow twisting streets with their little shops, mostly run by Indians, gay with bright silks and embroideries, past the magnificent wooden doors studded with enormous brass knobs. We drove past the royal palace but we did not see the King in his red Rolls-Royce car. We admired the wealthy Arabs, often handsome men in rich white clothes with jewelled daggers in their belts, and we saw the house from which Livingstone set off on his famous journeys of discovery into unknown Africa. The market was a brilliant blaze of colour, but some of the people resented being photographed. On a subsequent visit some years later our cameras nearly caused a riot and the police moved in to stop it, and us. There was much obvious poverty among the negroes in Zanzibar, very much the under-dogs, ruled by the Arabs. The upheaval of recent years, deplorable though it was, is to some extent understandable though no one could condone the excesses which have taken place. The old romantic atmosphere must now have gone forever and it is sad to think that we can never see it as it was, and had been for centuries. Today Zanzibar has a neglected and deserted air about it and we wonder how it can recover.

Moçambique came next on our African Odyssey, in the shape of Beira, a large modern port but not a particularly attractive town. Lourenço Marques, further down the coast, we found far more interesting, a truly modern city with many fine buildings, some interesting architecture and delightful mosaic patterns on nearly all the side-walks. The Portuguese have really gone to town on this capital city of Moçambique, making it a miniature Lisbon but even more modern. Some of us went to a type of night club on the outskirts of the city, where a feature seems to be that local Portuguese men may ask lady visitors for a dance without any preliminary introduction. It is all done in a most proper fashion, the men are excellent dancers and they return the ladies to their tables with a polite bow and gracious thanks, though communication is impossible if one does not know Portuguese.

In South Africa we stopped at four different ports—Durban, East London, Port Elizabeth and Capetown. We had two or three days in each and saw everything possible in the time. Durban is a fine modern city, set upon perfect sandy beaches, with vast rollers coming in off the Indian Ocean, a perfect place for surf riding. The most colourful feature here was the Zulu ricksha boys in their gorgeous costumes with patterns of beads, ostrich plumes and monkey skins. They compete with each other for the annual championship for the best dressed ricksha boy.

We saw much more of South Africa on our next visit, three years later, but Capetown completely fascinated us. It is surely one of the most beautiful sites for any city in the world, with its lofty mountain background, its wild and rocky coastline interspersed with superb beaches, and its flower-filled hinterland. It brought back happy memories for me from my war time visit many years earlier. It is a city we shall always be glad to see again.

After leaving Capetown we were homeward bound, with only three stops. The first was at St. Helena where Napoleon spent his last days. It is a beautiful rugged island with a pleasant climate, and the great soldier lived in Longwood, a large rambling house. He had some of the paths through the lush gardens lowered so that he could walk without being seen from nearby. We did not see what he had to complain about; we thought he was on to a good thing. He died on the island and his grave is still there, though his remains were taken to France some forty years after his death. Both the grave and the house are cared for by the French Government and are, indeed, really a little bit of France on St. Helena.

The natives of St. Helena are perhaps the most gentle, polite and friendly people in the world. They are a mixture of African, British and Portuguese, being a light brown in colour and speaking with a soft and musical tone, a rather quaint and old-fashioned English. The women make and sell lace but they never press their wares on visitors as is so often the case. They are quite delighted if you take an interest in their lovely children, and thrilled though bashful if you want to take a photograph of them. There are roads up into the hills, often lined with gorze and heather brought from Britain. The main crop grown is New Zealand flax, really a type of sisal, and that is their main export. The people are poor and the whole economy depends on grants from Britain. Few ships call there now, so it is a lonely island. But I would just delight in being marooned there for a few months. It would really be an island where you could get away from it all, a wonderful place in which to write a book in peace and quietness.

We called briefly at Ascension Island, a grim looking peak out in the middle of the South Atlantic. We could not go ashore but a sturdy launch came out to our ship, bringing with it a number of men and women from among the Cable and Wireless Company employees who operate a cable station there. The women flocked into the hair-dresser's shop on board for the rare luxury of a hair-do while the ship unloaded a variety of cargo and took on a few mysterious pieces. The men were an interesting group, glad to be able to talk with strangers and to have a drink in the bar.

This is another island I would love to explore. It is so rugged all round the coast that it looks impossible to land there at all. But there is a small cove and even a beach, though bathing would be sheer suicide because of sharks and is strictly forbidden. The company staff run a vegetable garden on the top of the peak, where clouds often rest and where there is some rain. Otherwise, the whole island seems to be barren lava and rock, a grim place to be stationed. The crew of our ship dropped fishing lines overboard, with small hooks totally devoid of any kind of bait. Immediately they began to haul on board small dark grey fish which were soon flapping about all over the decks. These are so voracious that they snap at empty hooks regardless and get themselves caught in dozens. It seemed to be good rapid sport, though I don't think the fish were edible.

We had a day at Las Palmas, on Grand Canary, and were taken on a trip into the mountains. This so intrigued us that we made plans not long after our return to visit the Canaries specially, giving ourselves enough time to explore them more thoroughly. We have been back now more than once and can never get enough of them. We like Teneriffe best of all, but both the main islands provide some exciting motoring on quite good roads. Lanzarote is entirely volcanic, with hundreds of extinct craters, steam and hot air spouts and all kinds of queer formations. The winds are sometimes so scorching hot that the vines, from which excellent wines are made, are planted in hollows in the black lava soil and protected by low stone walls.

And so, after ten weeks, our voyage around Africa came to an end. We had left in March and came home in mid-June. It was a glorious summer day when we landed and we shall never forget the sheer beauty of the English countryside from the train as we sped from Southampton to London. This has struck us time and again, so that for all the strange beauties we see in other countries, we still think Britain takes a lot of beating. In summer time, anyway.

CHAPTER TEN

South Africa and Rhodesia

I have already described the many ways in which our pictures of this around Africa trip were used, the articles we wrote, the big exhibition which toured the country, sponsored by Ilford Ltd. and the thousands of pictures which went into our library, helping to swell it to a respectable size. Let us return to southern Africa, as we did four years later, and I will describe our experiences in motoring for ten thousand miles from Capetown all the way to Victoria Falls, and back again by a different route. It took longer than the Around Africa trip and it yielded thousands of new pictures and many a subject for articles.

Union Castle asked us to travel outwards tourist class and to return first class, so that we could experience both types of travel on their ships. This worked out well, especially the luxury of first class on the way home after our long and sometimes arduous wanderings in southern Africa. We took many pictures on board both ships, and again at Las Palmas and at Madeira on the way home.

Before leaving on this trip to South Africa, I approached several big industrial firms for whom I had done photography, to see if there was anything I could do for them in southern Africa. Most responded eagerly. They would like photographs taken of their installations in Africa but it would not have been worth their while to send a photographer there specially. I was going to be there anyway, so they were glad to make use of my services.

I undertook several commissions for Shell, of factories and other places where their fuel or lubricating oils were used. Another firm, Mavor and Coulson, who made conveyor belt systems, wanted me to take photographs of as many different substances being carried on their belts as we could find. They had a factory in South Africa and so I went to see the manager there first. In the end we found ten different subjects, from various ores, diamonds, gold, chrome, platinum, and so on, to grain in a huge silo outside Pretoria. With letters of introduction, I called upon these various mines or factories as I went along. I had to do little driving off my route, and so my clients did not have to pay much in the way of my travelling expenses.

The General Electric Company wanted photographs of a big new power station recently opened in Bloemfontein, and also, by way of contrast, the lighting system they had installed in a newly built Greek Cathedral in Salisbury. An associated company had installed an automatic signalling system on the railway through Rhodesia and they asked me to photograph the main equipment near Wankie. I also did some photography for the Marconi Company of a new transmitting station in South Africa and again of some of the most modern ship's radio equipment, installed on the Union Castle liner on which we returned to England. I could take all these jobs in my stride as we went along. They not only added some useful subjects to our own library but they brought in an immediate return and indeed much more than paid all the expenses we had to bear ourselves on the whole four months' trip.

We duly arrived in Capetown, after a leisurely two weeks at sea and settled down in the Mount Nelson Hotel, standing in beautiful gardens below the slopes of Table Mountain. We took a lot of new pictures of the city and surrounding country, then I went off to Alexander Bay to do a job for Shell, while Betty photographed parts of Cape Town. Alexander Bay is situated in Namaqualand, at the mouth of the Orange River which forms the southern boundary of South-West Africa, and here the South African Government operates a diamond recovery plant. These are alluvial diggings, not a diamond mine; the diamonds are found in the gravel along the sea shore, doubtless washed down the river long years ago. Shell supplied much of the oil they used, hence pictures were required of the whole operation. I flew up there on an internal air service, with a man from Shell South Africa, and we spent several days going over the whole plant.

It was an extraordinary set-up. Prospecting was going on continually for many miles along the coast but the actual workings, including living quarters for a thousand people, were all enclosed in a huge double barbed wire fence. Neither blacks nor whites, about equal in numbers, were allowed out of this compound for six months, until they went on leave, except for about the half dozen top management men. Armed police guarded the only gate and positively no one was allowed in or out without a very special permit. My name was added to the list, and my Shell companion's, for the few days we were there. The point was, of course, that diamonds are very small objects and are easily smuggled. The best way to prevent smuggling was to keep everyone inside the compound.

But it did not seem like a concentration camp. There were nice houses, shops, schools, a hospital, recreation grounds, gardens and swimming pools, canteens and a market, as well as a poultry establishment, a dairy with many cows, and a market garden. A cinema, club houses and so on took care of leisure hours for everyone. It was all so large that the wire fence was hardly seen from most parts of it. The complete diamond recovery plant was in this compound and, naturally, the diamond house, the place where the recovered diamonds were kept. They were not particularly strongly guarded. The man in charge took me inside to take photographs and then brought a tray of rough gems out into the sunlight for more pictures. The tray held some fourteen thousand carats of diamonds, worth about £350,000, a six weeks' collection.

Outside the diamond house was a large boulder known as the Merensky Stone. Merensky was a diamond prospector and he, along with other men, went down to Alexander Bay in the 1920's to see what they could find. It was known that there were diamonds along that shore, but it was so remote that little prospecting had been done. These prospectors found no diamonds along the actual shore, near the waves, as they might well have expected to do. Merensky, it is said, went back a way and sat down to think. He noticed three terraces on the wide sloping beach and he realized that they were former tide marks, as it were, and that the land had risen over the centuries. If there were no diamonds on the wave-washed beach today, there might be some on these former beaches, he argued. And he started looking. He found some diamonds almost immediately and realized that his theory was correct. He lifted one boulder and found a natural declivity underneath it. Now diamonds are heavy and they tend to get washed into hollows. Merensky sat down and began to prod. Before he finished he had nearly five hundred diamonds from that one hole. The boulder was kept as a historical object of no mean interest, and named the Merensky Stone. It is reported that he sold his interests on the coast for a million and a half pounds sterling to the Government. The Government operates these diggings, controlling the output each year so as not to upset the diamond market and cause prices to drop.

Through the good offices of Union Castle, I had arranged to hire an Austin car from African Car Hire, as it then was, for the whole of our trip. They were delightful people to deal with and the car behaved perfectly for the whole ten thousand miles we drove it. Our route, without going into too much detail, consisted first of driving to Durban along the Garden Route, then north through Zululand and Swaziland to Barberton, further north through the whole of the Kruger National Park, on into Southern Rhodesia, through Bulawayo and the Wankie Game Reserve to Victoria Falls. From here we turned south again, returning to Cape Town via Bulawayo, Shabani, Gwelo, Salisbury, Inyanga, Umtali, Melsetter, Zimbabwe, Pretoria, Johannesburg, the Drakensberg Mountains, Bloemfontein, Kimberley and the Karoo. I will pick out some of the highlights of this three months' trek.

The Garden Route runs between Capetown and Durban, through much beautiful country, up into lofty hills and then along the coast. It really starts at Mossel Bay, going north, but many people regard the whole distance as the Garden Route. South Africans boast that they can cover the entire route in two days, nearly twelve hundred miles. We took eleven days over it, and could have done with longer. There was so much to see.

At Oudtshoorn we visited an ostrich farm, an extraordinary place where they breed hundreds of ostriches for the tail feathers of the male bird. It was astonishing to see them herded together in big pens just like chickens, only somewhat larger. We drove out a few miles to see the Cango Caves, from which it is said that Rider Haggard received the inspiration that compelled him to write his famous book—*King Solomon's Mines*.

We stayed at Wilderness for a day, set upon a beautiful stretch of coast with several large lakes just inland, like big lagoons. Then on leisurely through Port Elizabeth, with its famous Snake Farm, and East London, into the Transkei, a huge area set aside for native development. From Umtata we were taken out by an official from the Native Affairs Department, into areas where tourists cannot go without special permission. Here we saw Tembu and Pondo natives living their normal lives, growing crops, making their own houses and so on. Our guide was well known to them. At one kraal he leaned against our car and spoke to them in their own language. He was actually reciting some of their poetry, folk stories, I gathered, and they were responding, their eyes shining, completely wrapped up in their ancient traditions. We kept a little distance away and just watched. It was quite a poignant situation.

At Kokstad we met an extraordinary African, a very rich man, known as Khotsa. He had been told we wanted to see him and he turned out in style to greet us, complete with many of his wives and children. When we were having our breakfast in the hotel he was announced. Being black, he was not allowed into the hotel, so we went out to meet him. He was a rather stout man of medium height, dressed in a long robe of gorgeous colours, with a half circle of women and children behind him—his family! It was said that he had more than twenty wives and countless children. The whole family had been brought out to greet us. As we arrived, he came forward, dropped on to his knees and grasped our hands. Meanwhile, his wives all started chanting and clapping their hands in unison. People going to work had difficulty getting past on the wide sidewalk, and we received a few knowing looks from some of them. Khotsa was obviously well known.

He took us to his house in a huge American car, while his wives and children were bundled into a truck and followed behind. The house was rather ornate outside, a large white bungalow, with all sorts of elaborate furnishings inside. It looked rather like a museum, with countless shelves holding glassware, some intricate and good, and lot of it cheap and cheerful, including some Edward VIII coronation mugs. He was immensely proud of his home and showed us everything. Not many words were spoken at first, but every time we took a photograph of him or his family, he said 'thank you very much.'

He had some fine race horses stabled near his house, and ran them on various race courses. In fact, he was said to have made his fortune from forecasting the results of races. He said he had second sight and could predict the winners infallibly. Many people, white as well as black, came to him for tips, for which he duly charged them. He claimed that he called upon the spirit of the great Paul Kruger. He was also a herbalist and was said to be the chief witch doctor to his tribe, all remunerative occupations. Certainly he must have amassed no small fortune. I met a bank manager who said that sometimes after a big race, Khotsa would put thousands of pounds into the bank, his own winnings, presumably, on his own account.

We spent some time with Khotsa, taking photographs in his home and outside. He was particularly pleased when we selected two of his children for pictures, really lovely looking children. Two of his wives made some tea and we sat with him drinking it. He was obviously tremendously pleased with our visit and we were finally seen off with much chanting, clapping and cheering.

From Durban I went out to a big sugar plantation and took many pictures for Shell of the whole process, from cutting the cane to the milling and production of sugar. It is an elaborate process, with much big machinery that made some good pictures. Then we went on to the Hluhluwe Game Reserve, famous for white rhinos, a species that was in danger of extermination but is now being preserved in various parts of Africa. This reserve is only sixty square miles in area and is fenced all round, unusual for any game reserve. There are no lions here and, as the white rhinos are not aggressive like their black cousins, visitors are allowed to leave their cars, but they must be accompanied by a native game warden. These men know the animals and can take visitors quite close to them. We saw several, including one group of three or four adults with a couple of young ones. A warden took me to within fifty yards of them and I got a number of pictures, then we retreated. The warden told me that the only danger was from the animals stampeding and running down visitors accidentally in their panic.

We saw many other animals in Hluhluwe, even one or two black rhinos, but we kept well clear of these. There was one tame giraffe and an ostrich, both of which could be approached quite closely. It is a beautiful reserve, in rolling hills covered with trees and brush. We stayed in the rest huts at Reserve Headquarters and went out in our car looking for animals from there. It would have been pleasant to spend a whole week amidst the beautiful scenery of Hluhluwe.

We went on northwards and entered the Protectorate of Swaziland, not a part of South Africa. This native territory, along with Bechuanaland and Basutoland, was at that time administered by the Commonwealth Relations Office, through a High Commissioner stationed in the capital Mbabane. We stayed there, in a good hotel, with distant views over rolling mountains. This is a well watered country, often extremely beautiful, with large rivers and lush meadows. I went to a pineapple canning factory to do more photography for Shell, a very modern place.

One day a member of the High Commissioner's staff took us out to the Queen's kraal, where the old Queen Mother lived. She was not a very prepossessing looking woman, rather fat and old, and we had to drink native beer with her. The kraal was interesting, with beautifully woven round huts, very clean and tidy. The men were true warriors, armed with spears and looking very war-like. We were asked if we would give a young man a lift to the road when we left. He was in European dress—a sports jacket and open-necked shirt. He turned out to be a prince, heir to the throne of the paramount chief. He was a nice young chap, well educated abroad, very different in appearance to the warriors. We were duly honoured to carry a prince in our car.

High up in the mountains, at Pigg's Peak, a big afforestation programme was well under way. A fast-growing pine was being planted over some sixty-thousand acres, from which chip-board would be made. I had to visit the chip-board mill for Shell. Thinnings were already being used, the ten year old trees being then some twenty feet high. The trunks and branches were ground up into chips which were sandwiched between two sheets of hardboard, then cooked in big ovens. The natural gums and resins in the wood melted and acted as a sort of cement, so that when the 'sandwiches' were cooled, they became rigid, forming an excellent building board with good insulating qualities. From a high mountain top, the extent of the new forest was most impressive, stretching as far as we could see for miles in every direction.

Gold mining was another industry, of long standing, in Swaziland and, in more recent years, asbestos, with a big mine and mills at Havelock. Since we were there, iron ore mining has started in a big way, so that this little country is by way of being quite wealthy in natural resources.

We were heading north all the time, and from Barberton, where we were entertained to dinner by the mayor, and taken all round the neighbourhood the next day, we entered the Kruger National Park. This huge game reserve, as large as Wales, was inaugurated by President Kruger in 1898, a remarkably early case of game preservation in what was then a wild and savage land, sparsely populated. Today it stretches two hundred miles northwards along the frontier with Moçambique, as far as the Limpopo River, with an average width of some forty miles. We stayed at several of the Rest Camps, conveniently situated throughout the Reserve.

As we entered the Park we had a small bet as to which of us would spot and call out the first of each of the big animals. Soon a giraffe strolled across the road in front of us, stopped and looked down upon our car from only a short distance away. We were both spellbound and neither of us called out. Similarly, when we saw our first elephant we both forgot to call out, and in the end, neither of us won a single bet.

I can think of nothing so exciting and completely satisfying as driving about among the wild animals in Africa. These are no zoo animals, nor safari park captives. They are completely wild, free to go where they like, inside the park or out of it, living their natural lives for all to see. They have enough sense to know that they are safer within the boundaries of the park than outside it, despite a certain amount of poaching, and they stay there but wander far afield looking for their food, whether it be good grazing or other animals on which they prey, and of course regularly visiting the water holes. That is where they are most often found in large numbers.

Whenever we saw a small collection of cars stopped on the road, it denoted lions. Everyone wants to see lions, above everything else, and no one ever drives past them. They are quite unafraid of cars and never seem to attack people in them. Windows can be opened and the lions can be viewed from only a few yards away. One lioness walked close beside our car and yawned almost in my face as she passed. Others just sat on or near the road, quite indifferent to the cars and the chatter of the people in them. In recent years, lions have taken advantage of the cover provided by cars and done some stalking among them, occasionally pouncing on some poor innocent gazelle that had also lost its fear of cars and humans, and thought itself safe among the machines. People have actually seen a kill within a few yards range.

Elephants are not nearly so trusting. Visitors are advised not to go close to them, not to annoy them by making any noises such as revving the car motor or sounding the horn, and above all, always try to be in front of them, never to be faced by them on a road. This, of course, is not so easy on narrow tracks among bush and tall trees, as I discovered myself.

We were staying at Letaba Camp which is in elephant country, a district of scattered trees and forest. Elephants love to eat the leaves on the tops of trees. When they cannot reach them, they try to knock the trees down. Small ones are easy but sometimes larger trees are more difficult to fell. The elephant will first try to knock a tree down by pressing hard with its head against the trunk. If this fails, even by rocking the tree to and fro, the great pachiderm will turn its behind to the trunk and push again. It is quite a tree that can resist this enormous pressure. All round the Letaba Camp it looked as though a cyclone had swept through the trees. There seemed to be more on the ground than standing up. All the firewood used in the camp was obtained from these fallen trees; it was never necessary to cut any down or bring any wood in from other sources. We often heard the sudden crash of a falling tree as we drove along the roads from Letaba.

I stood one night beside the high wire fence round this Rest Camp, and listened to the animal noises in the darkness. Lions were roaring far off and there were all sorts of grunts and calls and mutterings, some well away, others seemingly quite close. I could hear elephants straining at trees, the creaking of the trunks and occasionally a sudden loud crash as one was pushed over. Immediately afterwards there was always a rumbling noise, obviously the elephant expressing its satisfaction at another conquest.

I went out alone one afternoon to look for elephants, hoping to do a round trip of some dozen miles or so through the forest country. I started out along a road through the trees that ran parallel to a large river, where elephants often went down to drink in the early afternoon. They would then wander slowly back across this road and lose themselves among the trees, feeding as they went. I soon saw my first elephant, a hundred yards or so away. He took no notice of me. Then I saw another one, on the river side of the road and I stopped. He looked at me, flapping his huge ears, moving a little way first one side and then the other. I could not understand this until he suddenly crashed through the bushes and ran across the road just behind my car. All he had wanted to do was to cross the road. I had my camera in my hand all this time, of course, taking an occasional picture with a medium telephoto lens. I immediately turned round and managed to get in one shot through the rear window of the car as the elephant ran past. It was one of the best elephant shots I ever secured.

I went further along this forest road, seeing an occasional elephant, and once a lion sitting on a rock across the river. Rounding a curve I suddenly spotted three elephants on the road in front of me, perhaps two hundred yards away. They were peacefully feeding and they ignored me. But they were in front of me and the road was too narrow to turn in. I stopped and waited, the motor running, the car in gear and my foot holding the clutch out, all highly advisable when elephants are nearby.

I had waited quite a while, until two of the elephants had disappeared into the bushes. I had one fleeting moment of madness when I contemplated rushing forward, hoping to scare the one off the road and getting by. It would have been sheer madness, just the thing one is advised not to do. At that moment one of the missing ones appeared again, a salutary warning to me not to be reckless. Then, through the open window on the other side of the car I heard a rustling noise and saw, to my alarm, a huge elephant standing eating not fifty yards away. My heart missed more than a beat, I hastily got into reverse gear and shot backwards for some distance. That was a bit too close for comfort. I managed to turn the car round and went back slowly to the camp. But as I drove along I reflected that, if you treat elephants decently, they react in kind and will do you no harm. Act like a gentleman and the elephant will be a gentleman, or lady, too.

The game wardens did not agree. They declared that elephants are unpredictable. Get them scared enough and they are likely to rush up to a car, turn it over and perhaps kneel on it, crushing it flat. It is surprising, but this rarely happens and there are few reported cases of actual attacks by elephants, despite considerable provocation by some foolish visitors. But it might happen and so one should not take chances.

We spent a pleasant evening with Colin van Zyl, and R.A.C. patrol officer stationed at Letaba. He was out all day and every day in the whole northern half of the Park and he expressed a healthy respect for elephants. He had never been attacked by one but he was quite definitely scared of them at close quarters, and after all, he should know. He told us a lot of interesting stories of his experiences.

One evening we had reason to call upon his services. We were returning from a day's outing near sunset time. Now it is a rule that all visitors must be back in their camp before sunset, when the gates are closed to keep animals out of the camp during the night. Anyone returning late is fined. We were within three miles of the camp, and within ten minutes of sunset, when we got a flat tyre. One is not allowed to get out of one's car except in a genuine emergency. This was one alright, but I knew there would not be time to change the wheel before sunset, and it gets dark very quickly there. There was a car behind us and we begged a lift to the camp, leaving our own behind.

The R.A.C. patrolman came out with me to rescue our car. It was quite dark by the time we could leave and he said that perhaps the elephants would be playing with it by the time we got there. But we found it in the headlights and it was unharmed. In the light of his headlamps we jacked up our car and changed the wheel. It was a strange sensation, imagining half the animals of the park standing around watching us, and perhaps contemplating an attack. But nothing happened and soon we were both driving our vehicles back to the camp. All sorts of animals watched us with glowing eyes, some running across the road in fright, but we got back safely.

In the Letaba Camp we sometimes came across Tommy's gazelles wandering about among the buildings and tents, but only at night. There was a herd of about fifty that spent every night in the camp, safely away from lions and other enemies.

They had learnt this themselves, always trooping daintily into the camp before the gates were closed at sunset, and waiting at dawn each morning to be the first out again. They were never late getting in.

We left the Kruger National Park at Punda Maria, at the north end and made our way across country to Beit Bridge and so into Southern Rhodesia, as it then was. The countryside seemed empty for many miles, just scrub country, dry and deserted. But nearer Bulawayo big ranches appeared, with cattle grids on the road and many native kraals. Bulawayo was surprisingly large and modern, with an enormously wide main street. It was said that Cecil Rhodes ordained that the main street should be wide enough to turn a span of oxen in it without the traces getting tangled, and a span was sixteen animals in pairs, usually pulling a covered wagon.

From Bulawayo we went out to the Matopos Hills to see Cecil Rhodes' grave carved out of solid granite, and we had a picnic lunch beside the lovely Malene Dam. Then we went on to Wankie, and into the Wankie Game Reserve. The entrance is near Dett, a small station on the railway line and this is where I had to photograph the newly installed railway signalling equipment. One of the main reasons why the system was required was because elephants were always knocking down the telegraph and signal posts along the railway. The new system used buried cables, which fooled the elephants. The other reason was to speed up the traffic on the railway and this it succeeded in doing to a remarkable degree.

The chief game warden, Davies by name, was stationed at the headquarters entrance near Dett. He took me out one day to sit by a water hole, while Betty went on to the Robins Camp at the northern end with some friends, and we met up later. Davies believed in comfort while watching nature. He carried two folding canvas chairs in his little truck and we sat in them later for hours, in complete comfort. He had an African boy with him and on the way out we cut some branches from bushes and low trees. At the waterhole, which was about a hundred yards across, he made a screen of the branches and we sat behind it, only our heads visible. There was a big tree overhead, and the boy climbed up it to keep a look-out. We forgot about him.

It was a beautiful spot, with birds singing and coming down to drink. Butterflies in considerable variety fluttered about. Davies was most knowledgeable about most things in nature and he whispered the names of the birds and butterflies as they appeared. After a while we saw a giraffe approaching slowly from the far side, then six zebras, not to speak of monkeys and the comical wart hogs. I had three cameras, all set and focused correctly and I laid them on the ground beside me. I also had a 16 mm cine camera, likewise prepared, with colour film in it. My idea was to pick up each camera in turn without moving my head, the only part of me that the animals could see, raise it gently to eye level and shoot without any other movement. I left the cine camera to the last, as it would be noisy.

It was so still and quiet that every tiny sound was audible. We could distinctly hear the beating of a butterfly's wings as it sailed past close to our heads. A dead leaf fell out of the tree and landed on the ground with almost a thunderous crash.

The animals were very wary at first, but thirst overwhelmed them in the end and we had seven animals in the water, with others just behind. I raised one camera and took a shot. Immediately, every head was raised in alarm. But as we kept perfectly still, they settled down again. This happened with each camera in turn. When I had the still pictures I needed, I reached for the cine camera. As soon as it started to whirr there was absolute panic. The giraffe and the zebras stampeded out of the water in a cloud of spray, while sundry buffalo and other animals approaching the water turned and ran, the whole lot disappearing in a cloud of dust. Marvellous action for cine work and it came out well. Davies stood up:

'Well, that's all for today at this water hole.'

Immediately his boy, up the tree above us, called out that a herd of elephants had been approaching from our side and had stampeded when they saw us and heard us moving. What a chance we missed, but I have often wondered what would have happened if they had come down to the water hole on our side.

The road to Robins divided into two branches, coming together again at the camp. We tossed as to which way we should go and saw no animals of note at all. Betty and our friends, having gone the other way, had seen elephant, buffalo and a pride of twenty lions including a number of young ones. The luck of the draw.

The next day Davies took me out to find the buffalo. He said they would not have gone far. As we were riding along a high bank above a small dried-up river course, we spotted a large herd of buffalo down below us.

'Let's go and look at them,' Davies said, and turned his Landrover down the bank and through enormously high grass towards the herd. He drove up on to a small knoll, standing a few feet above the grass. All round us were hundreds of buffaloes, in small groups and large, all looking our way, snorting, stamping, obviously disturbed.

'What about a stampede?' I asked.

'In all my years as a warden,' Davies replied, 'I nave never seen a stampede of buffaloes. They will run, but away from danger, not towards it. No, we are quite safe here.'

It was a thrilling experience being in the midst of those great beasts with their enormous thick horns. Davies calculated that there were probably a thousand of them altogether. They came nearer to us in small groups, then panicked and ran back. A large group, several hundreds of them, suddenly ran away in one great wave. All we could see as they disappeared, was the high grass bending as though in a tidal wave. We left these magnificent animals to their feeding and from the river bank we could see them settling down again.

As you approach the Victoria Falls, across a wide expanse of flat bush country, there is no sign of the great Zambesi River. Betty had gone on ahead of me again, while I spent the day in the Wankie coalmine, taking photographs above ground and below. It is a huge coal deposit, with the main seam more than thirty feet thick and only a couple of hundred feet below ground. I walked down to the coal face through a gently inclined shaft. The coalfield is said to be four hundred square miles in area and to contain four thousand million tons of coal. Only a tiny part has so far been developed and yet this one mine supplied virtually all the coal for half a dozen countries in south central Africa.

As I approached the Falls, wondering when I should see them, I suddenly spotted a huge white cloud sitting on the ground some miles away. This was the spray from the falls, rising a thousand feet above the gorge into which the entire river tumbles. The gorge lies across the path of the river which is here a mile wide, so the enormous volume of water has to turn at right angles along the gorge as soon as it reaches the bottom. Close to the falls a road and railway bridge crosses the gorge, nearly always smothered in spray, so that rail passengers get a marvellous view from the train.

We stayed for several days at the Victoria Falls Hotel, a mile or so away, and rested up before starting the second half of our long trek, back to Capetown. We took scores of pictures of all aspects of the falls, of the rain forests in the spray (a wet job, this) and we climbed down into the gorge itself. We flew over the falls in a small plane, and for sixty miles along the Zambezi River above them, at zero height. The pilot had to dodge the islands and clumps of trees as they loomed up ahead of us. Every now and then he pointed and shouted and we saw herds of elephants drinking, or hippos splashing in the water. Another day we flew far over Bechuanaland, seeing great herds of animals which often panicked at the noise of our plane. A game warden took us in his high speed launch up the river, to Kandahar Island, where elephants sometimes appear unexpectedly among the visitors, having swum over from the river banks.

We drove back to Bulawayo again, then on to Selukwe and to Gwelo, where I took a lot of photographs of the Ferrochrome steelworks, a very modern plant making special hard steel. I was interested to see Africans handling molten steel and manipulating complicated machinery in what looked to me a most professional manner. One of the managers told me that, when they take on raw recruits, some of them panic as soon as they see all the sparks and fire and molten metal and head straight out for the bush never to return. Others are fascinated by it all and many of them become quite skilled in their work, not at all afraid of it.

Salisbury, the capital of the Federation at that time, and now of Rhodesia proper, was a fine modern city with many tall buildings. I have not seen it since then but I believe I would hardly recognize it, it has grown so much. We stayed there for several days and then drove eastwards to the mountains along the border with Moçambique, a very different type of country altogether.

As we neared the mountains, it grew cloudy and rainy and we ran into mist in the heights. We stayed at the Troutbeck Inn at Inyanga, operated by the man who formerly ran the Troutbeck Inn in the Lake District. It was near a lake, amidst rolling hills that were very like Scotland, with bracken and heather and many flowers. The next day we drove up to the edge of a huge escarpment which drops sheer for thousands of feet, at the spot known as World's View, with unbelievable views. We would gladly have spent a week or more at Inyanga. There was a golf links, a bathing pool and some wonderful trout fishing in nearby streams.

We went on to Umtali and stayed at the Christmas Pass Hotel, run by a lady we had met in Skye a few years before. She was a MacLeod and her house was called Dunvegan. She took us up into the Vumba Mountains, vast rolling downlands with enormous views far away into distant blueness, marvellous country with a splendid climate, as it is several thousand feet above sea level. For many miles after we turned south from Umtali we were travelling through these highlands, past great wattle plantations, through the lovely farming district of Melsetter, on to the Chimanimani Mountains. Beyond Melsetter we drove through lofty ranges of mountains where a man operating a petrol station gave us a big bag of tangerines, just because he liked the look of us, presumably.

At last we dropped down out of the lush green mountains to the hot dry plains below where gross, thick-trunked baobab trees were a great feature. They have short branches and enormous swollen trunks, actually half full of water. Many a man lost in this type of dry country has saved his life by knowing that he could tap water from baobab trees. We crossed the Birchenough Bridge and went on to the mysterious ruins at Zimbabwe. No one knows who built them nor how old they are, but they are most impressive, like a great fortress standing in open country.

The next day we reached the Beit Bridge again, and crossed the Limpopo River back into South Africa. We drove through beautiful hilly country, through great forests and past big orange groves. And so on to Pretoria, the Administrative Capital of South Africa, a fine city, worth visiting, in our opinion, to see the Voortrekker Monument alone, a magnificent example of modern-day sculpture.

Johannesburg is a must in any visit to South Africa. Not that it is particularly beautiful but it is unique. It is surrounded by enormous tailings dumps, the refuse from the gold mines which were responsible for the very foundation of this, the largest city in South Africa. But these mine dumps are not eye-sores; they are golden in colour and are quite attractive in their way. Gold is still mined here, and much further afield, and is easily South Africa's most important industry, accounting for eighty percent of the free world's production.

The great thing to do on a Sunday morning is to go out to one or other of the big mine compounds and watch the native dancing. This is put on by the various tribes of Africans working in the mine. They dress up in either their traditional native costumes, which are most colourful and elaborate, or in some modern concoction which they originate themselves, with gumboots, tee shirts and almost anything. They vie for the greatest applause from the audience, and this is one of the rare places where there are both blacks and whites in the audience at the same time. We would not have missed this for anything.

While I was in South Africa this time I gave several lectures to photographic societies. One was at Witwatersrand University in Johannesburg. Our host on the occasion, a man who took us around and showed us a lot of the city and district, was Dr. Bensusan, a great pictorialist who has often exhibited in the London Salon of Photography. The University, in those days, was one of the few places where whites and blacks and coloureds could mix freely. Bensusan was a liberal-minded man and he arranged for my lecture to be given at the University so that he could ask members of 'coloured' photographic societies to be present. Actually, only some of the Chinese turned up, but at least we could all meet together and discuss photography. During the interval Dr. Bensusan suddenly said to Betty:

'Tell us what it is like to be a photographer's wife.'

Taken totally unawares, Betty stood up and gave them the best part of ten minutes' talk about her part in the team and how she coped with everything, from cooking at home to photography abroad. It went down well.

In that year—1956—there was much trouble in Sophiatown, a native housing area. The Government wanted to move the Africans further out of town and develop this area for white housing. I thought it would be interesting to see Sophiatown and asked various people if it would be possible. The general answer was:

'It would be madness. Quite impossible, I wouldn't go down there on a bet. But if you are tired of life, try it!'

I mentioned it to Bensusan. He jumped at the idea, and told us that he often went there, that he had friends among the Africans and he would take us down the following Sunday afternoon.

We drove down in his car and parked in one of the streets, then walked about. This was a rest day and the people were lounging about out of doors. We were received in a most friendly way, though we were something of a curiosity. Not many white people went into Sophiatown, that was plain to see. The people smiled at us and gave us a greeting. A few even invited us to go into their houses, most of which were primitive shacks in various stages of decay. A few of the people recognized Bensusan and we stopped to talk with them. Children crowded round and wanted to be photographed. Some of the smaller children were beautifully dressed, in their Sunday best. Their parents glowed with pride when we selected them for pictures. There was not the slightest sign of animosity towards us anywhere.

We heard a band playing nearby and Bensusan uttered one word 'wedding'. We hurried across a vacant lot and there was a procession coming down the street, the bride and groom, formally dressed in long tails, top hat, long white dress and veil—the real thing. I got ready to take a photograph. The procession stopped, the people gathered into a formal group in the middle of the street and they were thrilled to be photographed by white people. It undoubtedly made their day, and crowned their wedding. I sent them some pictures after our return home.

Some of the young men had formed a golf club and made a rough sort of golf links nearby. Bensusan knew a few of them and we all trooped across to take some action pictures. There were some splendid types among these people, girls as well as men, and we had a long and friendly talk with them after the golf. I told the Union Castle man, and other people we had met in Johannesburg, where we had been and they were frankly incredulous. They said they would not dare to go.

Now we set off across country again, to stay for a few days at Mont aux Sources in the Drakensberg Mountains—the Royal Natal National Park. These mountains form a huge block with a great escarpment standing ten thousand feet above sea level in the form of a vast amphitheatre. Mont aux Sources, with its beautiful hostel in the centre of the valley some five miles from the rock wall, is ideally situated amidst gardens and pools and countless wild flowers. The hostel consists of a number of chalets with a central building containing the dining room. There was a plaque on our chalet saying 'occupied by His Majesty King George VI. 13th—17th March 1947.'

Others had plaques commemorating the fact that Queen Elizabeth and Princess Elizabeth had slept in them.

One day I drove the car as far as I could and then walked seven miles to the foot of the cliffs, past waterfalls, across streams and through woodlands and scrub country and smooth green swards. It was a long day but very well worth while. There is an ambitious trail for miles along the peaks forming the top of the great cliffs, and all sorts of easier trails, on foot or horseback.

After the Drakensberg Mountains we turned resolutely southwards for Capetown, first stopping in Bloemfontein for a couple of days. Here I covered the power station for the General Electric Company. I saw the pictures taken by a local photographer and realized at once that what was required was a high viewpoint. He had stayed at ground level, from where he could not hope to cover the vast generators and turbines. I finally got up on the travelling crane which ran the length of the building. There is always one of these in a power station. It is essential for lifting the machinery into place and for removing any parts of it that may require later work or repairs.

I signalled to the crane driver to stop when I had reached a good vantage point, then put my camera on a short tripod and proceeded to take time exposures in existing light, perhaps two to five seconds. These turned out quite well, giving quite a dramatic picture of the whole installation.

We went on to Kimberley where we were the guests of the town, which is virtually de Beers, the diamond people. A prominent citizen met us and told us that they did not think they had a good enough hotel in the town so he was putting us up in his house. We would be free to go out each day and do our work without any obligation towards him and his wife. Whenever we turned up again they would be glad to see us and we would eat at their house. This scheme worked very well. I went all over the diamond workings, taking lots of pictures. We both went into the Diamond House and were entertained to lunch by de Beers. Then we photographed the selecting and weighing of diamonds, in rooms where the public are never allowed to go. Not surprising, considering that some five million pounds worth of diamonds were lying around in them. Betty plunged her hand into half a million pounds worth of rough diamonds while I photographed her, and no one searched us afterwards.

Diamondiferous gravel, or the blue clay of Kimberley, really a volcanic chimney coming up from the depths of the earth and containing diamonds, is broken up and reduced to a slurry with water. This is passed through concentrated chemical solutions which float off the lighter rocks and stones, leaving only what are known as 'heavies'. These, very much concentrated residues from the original gravel or clay, are then passed over grease tables, really sloping shelves covered with heavy grease like vaseline. Diamonds have the peculiarity of not holding water on their surfaces like other stones do. In other words, you cannot wet a diamond. It remains dry, as it were, even in water. Hence the grease grabs on to these dry stones, allowing all the other wet ones to slide off it. It is surprising how efficient this method of recovery is. Not a single diamond is ever lost, apparently. So efficient is it that old tailings from many years back—there were mountains of them all round Kimberley—were being retreated, and the diamonds recovered made it worth while.

We found Kimberley to be a bright modern little city, with many fine buildings among the old historical ones, which were being preserved, especially the original de Beers Building. A new civic centre was about to be built and the land would probably be gone over for diamonds first. They actually lie around everywhere, in theory at least, but no one is allowed to even look for them. If you find one by accident, leave it where it is. Report it if you like, but on penalty of a heavy fine, don't touch it. All diamonds belong to de Beers and if you brought a handful into them, you would soon be in serious trouble.

We had a wonderful time in Kimberley. The people were most friendly and hospitable, throwing parties for us and making us welcome everywhere. Many of the private houses were most attractive, and each garden seemed to be filled with citrus fruit trees—oranges, lemons and grapefruit. We were sorry to leave.

Our route southwards now lay right across the Karroo, a vast area of semi-desert, yet with enough vegetation to make it the great sheep-rearing district of South Africa. Some people consider it dull and dreary, to be got through as quickly as possible. We found it quite fascinating, with a beauty all its own. There were many flat-topped hills, stark and clear against the sky, and to us it was far from a desert. It was by then early Spring in South Africa and there were masses of wild flowers everywhere. Later these flowers make a wonderful show. The main road was excellent, like most of this country's highways, with very little traffic, and we averaged sixty miles an hour quite easily. The Karroo gives one an impression of vast open spaces, clean, wind-swept country, more than almost anywhere we have been. We enjoyed our five hundred miles across it.

We spent a couple of nights at Paarl, only some forty miles from Capetown. This is the centre of the wine industry, a beautiful stretch of country filled with green hills, vineyards and lush green valleys. Here again we were offered the hospitality of the town. They put us up in a fine old Dutch farmhouse, with a family who were so Afrikaans that they kept forgetting to speak English, apologising frequently to us for not remembering that we did not know their language. But they really looked after us extremely well, and one of them took us all over the surrounding countryside, to the vineyards and the wineries. We were touched with their warm hospitality and friendship.

We spent our last few days in Capetown, being invited to various parties in private houses, and even being interviewed on radio. We ourselves threw a cocktail party on the Union Castle ship in which we should be returning to

England, and invited many of the people who had helped us in so many ways and been so hospitable to us. We were surprised at the number who came and realized how many different people had helped to make our trip a success. We turned in our Austin car to African Car Hire and were greeted with surprise.

'Here comes the missing car,' someone said. 'We had forgotten all about it and thought it had got lost.'

We had grown quite used to it and were sorry to have to give it up. It had carried us everywhere with no trouble at all, on smooth roads and rough, in all sorts of country and we had found it completely reliable in every way.

As our ship was sailing, the recorded interview with us was put on the air. The radio operator lent us a portable radio set and we took it out on deck to listen. It was strange listening to our own voices. Betty's voice, I thought, was particularly good; I think she would make a most satisfactory radio announcer.

The fortnight's journey home was most pleasant. We just relaxed in sheer comfort after our long and often hard travels. I developed many of my black-and-white films in the cabin, to save time when I got home and we took many new pictures of life on board. Again we called at Las Palmas and this time at Madeira also, for a few hours, the basis for several more trips there in later years. Madeira has become one of our favourite islands, but that is another story.

CHAPTER ELEVEN

The Far East

We had done quite a bit of business with the British India Steamship Company, supplying them with pictures of East Africa and other parts of the world. Our chief contact there was Eric Smith, the Publicity Manager. One day early in 1958 he phoned me up.

'Allan, how would you and Betty like to go on one of our ships from Calcutta to Japan and back,' he asked. 'We need pictures on that route and we can't find any.'

My mind raced at the possibilities that loomed up, and of course I said yes. We needed everywhere in the Far East in our library and this suggestion made it look as though we could conquer a number of countries all in one trip. I went to see Eric and we began to plan.

British India could not get us out to Calcutta, but they are part of the vast P. and O. group, whom we had met at promotion parties. We had talked of going on P. and O. ships some time and they had said that a suitable opportunity would arise some day. This seemed to me to be the opportunity we had been waiting for. In those days P. and O. operated a wide network of passenger services, so I suggested that on the trip to Japan and back, wherever British India could not carry us, perhaps P. and O. could. They approved of the idea, so I got down to planning actual dates. This is one of the things I most enjoy—planning a complicated trip. I can spend hours on it, with maps and time tables, pen and paper. To me it is one of the joys of this profession.

We had not been to India so we discussed the possibility of going out to Bombay on a P. and O. passenger ship that would get us there several weeks before the B.I. ship sailed from Calcutta. The Indian State Tourist Corporation offered us some valuable concessions, though they could not offer us hospitality for the whole of the six weeks we proposed to spend in India. Indian Airlines co-operated in getting us about in India, as also did the Indian State Railways.

The B.I. ships from Calcutta stopped for only two days in Hong Kong, and this was not enough time for us. So I proposed stopping off there for ten days and going on to Japan on a P. and O. cargo ship. This was agreed upon and then the question of getting home from Japan arose. I did not want to do the return journey to Calcutta on the B.I. ship as it would merely be repeating what we should have done already by then. P. and O. had passenger ships sailing all the way home from Japan. They agreed to bring us home and asked what date we would want to leave Japan. I told them it would be about April 25th, the following year, as we planned to spend about a month in Japan. They looked up their time-tables and I saw a spark light up in the publicity manager's eye.

'This is most fortunate,' he said. 'On that very date the HIMALAYA sails from Kobe, and this will be the first time it has been in Japan. It has not been to Manila or Hong Kong either. Could you take pictures of the ship in these ports?'

Of course I could and I agreed at once.

'We would like pictures of this ship arriving at Manila and Hong Kong. Could you do this?' he asked.

'Yes, if you can arrange to have me taken off the ship before it lands', I replied. I knew how difficult this was because positively no one, not even the captain, is allowed off the ship until it has been cleared by the medical authorities at each port of call. He said he would see what could be done.

This meant that we should be arriving back at Bombay in mid-May, just at the right time of the year for Kashmir. We would have used up every possible conces-sion that the Indian tourist people, and Indian Airlines, could afford to give us by that time, so this extra trip would have to be at our own expense. I suggested leaving the HIMALAYA at Bombay and catching the next P. and O. ship home after that. It turned out to be a whole month later. Alright, we would spend a month in Kashmir. We might never have the chance again, so this was something we could not miss. Altogether we should be away from home for eight months. We had a manager in the office now, so the business did not need us there all the time. This whole trip was a chance in a lifetime.

We were to sail from London early in November, and from Calcutta early in February. A double cabin was reserved for us first class on the CARTHAGE, a famous old ship and a happy one. We looked forward to it. Then something else happened.

We received a request from Paddy Garrow-Fisher, who had pioneered coach trips in India, for pictures of all the countries through which his coaches travelled on this long and arduous route. We had hardly any, not having been to Turkey, Persia or anywhere further east. My manager came up with a bright idea.

'Why not take Mr. and Mrs. Cash with you on one of your trips. They would take all the pictures you need,' he suggested.

Paddy jumped at the idea, for he had a coach going to India in a few weeks time. We met him and went to a lecture he gave in London about a previous trip, illustrated with a film taken by one of his passengers. The more I saw of it, the more I thought this was just my cup of tea. Betty was not so sure. It would be a rough trip, camping out in remote parts, crossing swollen rivers, getting bogged down in sand in the Persian deserts, and so on. Betty preferred the comfort of a big passenger ship. She is a good sport and is always prepared to rough it where necessary. But she drew the line at this. The coach trip would take about nine weeks, if all went well.

'Why be uncomfortable for as long as that?' was Betty's philosophy. 'It is India we want, and countries further east, not the road to India.'

I thought quite differently. What a marvellous chance to get pictures of all sorts of remote places, and a whole string of new countries for our library. I agreed to go. The coach was to be a new one, specially built for the job, with air-conditioning and a special body that would stand up to the rough roads. We were supposed to start in mid-September but in fact the coach was not ready. We would be a month late starting. Then something else happened.

I had been writing to the Japanese Tourist Organization in Tokyo about our forthcoming trip, and they had promised help of various kinds. Suddenly I received an invitation from K.L.M., the Dutch Air Line, to go on a proving flight to, of all places, Tokyo. This would be over the North Pole, a trial flight, as it were, before they commenced a regular service a few weeks later. At that time only S.A.S. were flying the Polar Route. Now, of course, everyone does. I should be away eight days, leaving just one week after my return before I started on the coach trip to India. I accepted. I sent a cable to Tokyo saying I would be there in a few days and would call in to discuss our later trip to Japan.

We left Amsterdam for Tokyo late at night, made a short refuelling stop at Stavanger, in Norway, then set out on the fifteen hour flight to Anchorage, Alaska. This was before the days of jets; it only takes half as long today. We woke up early the next morning, almost exactly over the Pole, with the sun just rising, so we had breakfast. Then, two hours later, the sun set again, so we all went back to sleep.

We were a mixed bag of passengers, journalists, travel agents and K.L.M. officials, all invited, and it was all very much first class. The captain was English, a friendly chap who spent quite a lot of time with his passengers. He told us that, all the way across the Arctic wastes, we were never more than two hundred miles from a landing strip, either one of five Russian and American scientific stations on the ice, or Dewline (Distant Early Warning) radar stations that the Americans had set up all along the Arctic coasts. A comforting thought as we gazed down at vast stretches of ice floes far below us.

We were aroused for lunch as we crossed the coast of Alaska. It was still dark but the sun began to rise a second time, disclosing a stupendous wilderness of snow-covered mountains and valleys. We were to stay for a full day in Anchorage, as this was a proving flight and Alaska was not to be merely a refuelling stop. It was 2 p.m. Amsterdam time when we landed, but 7 a.m. Alaska time. So we went to our hotel and were offered breakfast! Later we had another lunch, and a gala dinner in the evening. The people of Anchorage gave us a wonderful time, then and on our return from Tokyo, when we spent another full day there. We were invited to parties in private homes, taken all round the countryside and feted like visiting royalty.

In Tokyo I phoned my contact at the Tourist Organization, took a taxi and spent a couple of hours poring over maps and arranging the trip that Betty and I would do in six months time. It was most useful. We were all taken on sight-seeing trips, to shopping centres and a judo wrestling hall, to temples and parks, and at night to a geisha banquet, Japanese style, squatting on the ground at low tables. A very useful introduction to Japan for me altogether.

On the way back, after our second day at Anchorage, we stopped at Lulea, in northern Sweden. K.L.M. wanted to find a suitable refuelling stop for this Arctic route. Stavanger was too near to Amsterdam. Lulea was better. It was an air force station and we were the first foreign plane ever to be allowed to land there. The officers took charge of us completely, literally rolling out a red carpet, giving us drinks and a snack, then taking us in a coach for a tour round Lulea. It was dark when we arrived at Amsterdam. I got a BEA plane immediately for London and was soon home. A week later I set off on my six months trip to Tokyo, but before leaving I was able to develop all my films and identify them, so that the office could use them while I was away.

The coach trip took nine and a half weeks from London to Delhi, but this included stops of two, three and even four days at various places en route. We went down to the south of France, along the Riviera into Italy, then right across Yugoslavia to Belgrade, into Bulgaria, then Turkey as far as Instanbul. We stopped off for a day or two in Paris, Venice, Belgrade, Sofia and for three days in Istanbul. I did this trip mostly because of these stops; I would not have been interested in it had it been a matter of driving on every day. The stops were invaluable to me and I had already accumulated a good bag of new pictures before we even got out of Europe.

Paddy himself drove the coach, and we started off in good style. But even before we left France the air-conditioning system had broken down. All the way to India bits and pieces kept falling off the coach, especially on the rougher roads further east. The chassis and motor were excellent; they were the same as used on London buses. But the body with all its fancy fittings was a dead loss. It just did not stand up even to smooth roads, let alone rough ones. Long before we reached India Paddy had stopped payments on it and eventually handed it back when he returned to London months later. But it got us to India, in spite of everything. It was comfortable to ride in and Paddy's Indian wife was able to cook food on board when necessary. Sometimes it was very necessary.

There were seventeen people on board, though it would have held thirty. We were a mixed bag. One young Australian returning home. An American couple on a trip round the world, another middle-aged American lady, an elderly New Zealand lady, a scientist on her way home, the wife of a tea planter in south India wanting a different way back to India, a young R.A.F. wife with a fourteen year old son on their way to Singapore, a nurse going to visit friends in the Persian Gulf, myself as a crazy journalist, and so on. We all got on well together, all the time. Paddy was a wonderful host, never down-hearted no matter what happened.

In Ankara we met another of his coaches, a pretty ancient affair, returning from India, with two drivers. He took over Albert, one of them, who was his permanent driver and came from Persia, speaking six languages. He had been a long distance truck driver in Persia and knew everyone on the roads. He and Paddy were both superb drivers and Albert was an excellent mechanic. Both were distinctly characters, each in his own way. We could not have asked for better companions. The only trouble with Paddy was that he was tireless; he never wanted to stop driving. We had to insist occasionally, when it got dark, as we wanted to see the country we were passing through. He reserved no hotels anywhere, but just took a chance. We had problems in some of the smaller places, especially in the remoter parts of Turkey and Persia, but always found something, and we could always camp out as a last resort. Actually, we should have done more of this but we had left rather late in the year and we ran into a lot of cold weather, with snow and ice in places for days on end.

In Sofia, thanks to my pre-war friend Alex Rizov, to whom I had written, the Bulgarian Tourist people took us in hand for a whole day, with a sight-seeing trip in their own coach, all round Sofia, up on to Mount Vitosha for a splendid lunch, then out into the country. I was persuaded to give a short talk to an English class at a girl's school, and I went to a political meeting with Alex in the evening. Two days later we arrived in Istanbul, known as Constantinople when I was a boy. I had not been there before and I certainly made the most of it. To me, this is one of the most fascinating cities in the world. I like it more every time I see it, like Venice and Hong Kong and a few more places.

I could write a whole book on this coach trip to India, but as this one has to cover a lot more, I must restrict myself to some of the highlights. We spent a day in Ankara, then went right along the Black Sea coast of Turkey, mostly in torrential rain and wild winds. From Trabzon we climbed up over the Pontine Mountains, in deep snow, and went on to Gulusane where a school master allowed us to sleep in his school, as the only hotel was unspeakable. We had a big party with all the teachers.

Near Erzerum we had to take on an armed guard, as we were in a military zone, near the Soviet border. Nearing the Persian frontier, we had magnificent views of Mount Ararat. The weather was cold and dry now for some days, with sharp frost each night and sometimes bitter winds during the day. It took several hours to cross the frontier from Turkey into Persia, thanks to bureaucratic officials and soldiers who obviously did not like us on the Turkish side. The Persians were much more friendly and gave us cups of sweet tea.

All the way across Persia, for two thousand miles, we were on mostly rough roads, often corrugated, which made bits and pieces fairly fly off our coach, until the luggage rack on the top became a tangled heap of metal. We were now in some of the wildest country I have ever seen, with bare rocky mountains, deep gorges and vast rolling hills dotted with huge flocks of sheep. It was cold and sunny and the whole countryside was extremely colourful. We had picnic lunches cooked on the coach, sitting out on the ground in the sunshine.

Teheran, we found, was a big modern city, with some superb ancient mosques and palaces and museums. But to me Isfahan was infinitely better. We spent three days there and explored every bit of the old city. The ancient Maidan is all enclosed within the old walls, such a vast area that there used to be a polo ground in the middle of it, with mosques and some lovely old buildings all around.

The mosques of Isfahan are exquisite beyond words, covered with brilliant mosaics. I managed to climb on to the top of one of them and got some unusual pictures. I called at the Christian Hospital, where my cousin had taught some years earlier, and where my uncle, as head of the Church Missionary Society, was well known. I got a great welcome and was invited to a reception for the visiting Bishop of Jerusalem one night. The next day I did a photographic story on the hospital and the man who ran it, Dr. Wild, a great character and a fine surgeon. It was later published in England and yielded some valuable publicity for the hospital.

Beyond Isfahan we were in real desert country, for hundreds of miles. We stayed at Yezd for a night, and at Bam. Here most of us had to sleep out of doors on the balcony of a small hotel, in our sleeping bags, as there was no room inside. We washed in warm mineral water next morning from a hydrant in the street below. Paddy drove out of town into the desert before we had breakfast, in case the police decided to collect our passports and show their authority, as had happened on a previous trip. I was almost arrested here for taking photographs and only just managed to hide my cameras in time.

Beyond Zahedan, at our last stop in Persia, we all slept out under the stars. It was much warmer now and this was sheer bliss. This was the day we had got badly stuck in wind-blown sand on the alleged road. It was quite miraculous how, as soon as we ground to a halt, we were surrounded by a band of wild looking natives, eager to dig us out. We wondered how much sand they had been piling on to the road before we arrived. They seemed to make a living digging out vehicles at this point, a nice little racket.

As soon as we crossed into Baluchistan, in Pakistan, we were on a good tarred road, evidence of British administration. More wild mountain country now, including the rugged Lak Pass leading up to Quetta, over five thousand feet above sea level, a green and pleasant city with—what utter bliss—a good hotel and a hot bath. And two days to rest up and explore this old town, formerly a military outpost of the British Empire. Then southwards to Karachi, with a day at the famous ruins of Mohenjodaro, Sir Mortimer Wheeler's happy hunting ground.

Karachi was big and noisy and we were glad to get out of it. We headed north-eastwards now for Lahore, through green cultivated land, irrigated by the waters from the great Lloyd Barrage across the Indus River. Then two more days to Delhi and my trip was over, though the coach went on to Bombay. Betty had arrived in Bombay two weeks earlier and had come up to Delhi to meet me. Our coach drove up to her hotel, the Janpath, and so we were reunited, after nearly two and a half months. She had been staying with some good friends of ours in Bombay and had done a lot of very useful photography there. We had a lot to talk about.

India is a continent in its own right, vast and diverse in its people, climate and scenery, from steaming tropical jungles and flooded paddy fields, to hot dry savannahs and the world's highest mountains, encompassing a wide range of people and religions. It is a country with problems of frightening immensity, from over-population, under-nourishment, poverty, starvation and ignorance to religious taboos and conflicts that appear insoluble. We saw a lot of it, on this and later occasions. We are always delighted with its beauties and its colourful cities, temples and fortresses and its kindly people; we are saddened at the poverty and the conflicts which create such appalling problems.

We flew and we motored and we went by train to many parts of India in the next six weeks. We explored all Delhi, the fine modern capital created by Lutyens, and the crowded fascinating old town, the Red Fort and all the other historical sites. We went to Agra and we saw the Taj Mahal by day and night, yes, even in full moonlight. It was not a disappointment. We found it more beautiful that we had believed possible. It is, surely, the most perfectly proportioned and exquisite building in the world. We went to Jaipur, so rightly called 'The Pink City', with its lovely palaces, its walls and ancient gateways all built from pink stone, and the flower markets along the streets, ablaze with deep golden marigolds, a religious flower widely used.

We went down to south India, largely thanks to the wife of the tea planter who had been on the coach from London. She invited us to stay with them at their big colonial house in Coimbatore, and they enabled us to see much of southern India from there. They sent a car for us to Bangalore and we drove across country through Mysore to two of their tea and coffee plantations before we even got to Coimbatore. From there we covered much of the Nilgiri Hills and we went down to Cochin and back by the Anamallais Hills. We photographed tea and coffee, hydro-electric plants under construction, all sorts of farming activities, rubber growing, towns and villages and festivals and people—a rich bag indeed. Our wide coverage of southern India owes much to their warm hospitality and generosity.

We went on by train to Madras, spent a few days there and then flew up to Calcutta. This is not India's most attractive city by far. The poverty hits one like a hammer blow. Perhaps half a million people live entirely in the streets, sleeping huddled on the pavements, cooking their rice on tiny fires and getting pushed out of sight during the day by the police, to return to the only home they know in the evening. No wonder Calcutta is a political hotbed and centre of vice. We covered its temples and its streets and lovely parks, and something of its people and the busy Hooghly River and docks.

I did a big story on a jute mill and I also spent a day at Durghapur, where a British consortium was erecting a huge steel works. This was a hard day, from 6 a.m. to 10 p.m., with over a hundred miles by road to Durghapur, and all day tramping round the half-built steel works in blazing heat. But these pictures sold well later, including a lot to the consortium itself.

We flew to Benares, now called Banaras, at the time of a great festival and were nearly swept off the famous ghats into the River Ganges, along with thousands of pilgrims who came to bathe in these holy waters to ensure their safe passage to Heaven when they die. We were rowed up and down the river, past many temples, past the burning ghats where human bodies were being burnt, and we struggled back up the endless wide steps among all the people going down to bathe. It was an incredible sight.

Back to Calcutta, it was time to board the British India ship SANTHIA, to sail for Hong Kong. It was a beautiful white ship, not large, being something under ten thousand tons. It carried all sorts of passengers, from a mere twenty five or so first class, to many hundreds below decks—peasants going to Malaya to work on plantations—who lived and cooked their food below decks and we only knew they were there when I went down to photograph them. I was told that the ship could carry as many as three thousand people altogether, including the various classes in between. Yet to us it was not crowded, and it was indeed a pleasant ship to be on.

We stopped first at Rangoon and we padded on our bare feet most of one morning all over the fabulous Shwedagon Pagoda, all gold and colour and intricate carvings. It had to be done in the morning because by lunch time the sun made the tiles too hot to walk upon. We explored every part of this tropical city, a most attractive place but to our regret there was not time to go inland, so that is all we saw of Burma.

Penang was next on the list, on the west coast of Malaya. It was one of the highlights of our whole trip, a lush tropical island of sheer beauty and colour. We bathed in the sea and found it too warm altogether, but the beach was superb, shaded by coconut trees and with coral sand as smooth as velvet.

At Singapore we met friends and were entertained and shown around largely by them. It was hot and sticky and tiring—how much better in more recent times when we found everywhere air-conditioned—but a fascinating city all the same. Two big P. and O. passenger ships were in at the same time, so the company hired a small plane for me to photograph them from the air. I covered the city as well before coming down, a chance not to be missed. As soon as I got back I was taken out on a Customs launch to photograph one of the ships sailing, all among the hundreds of vessels of every kind anchored in the vast harbour.

One day I watched a pilgrim ship, packed to the scuppers, sailing for Jeddah, with Moslems going to visit Mecca. A rainstorm burst upon us. I sheltered under someone's umbrella but it made little difference. Everyone was wet through in no time. But the sun soon reappeared and within a few minutes we were all dry again.

There followed seductive days of sheer laziness on tropical seas to Hong Kong, with cool breezes and sparkling seas, then quite suddenly a gale sprang up, the temperature dropped many degrees and the sun was replaced by cold grey clouds. In Hong Kong the central heating was turned on in our hotel.

The approach by sea to Hong Kong is superb, a long run through green and lofty islands, in sheltered waters, until the Peak looms up, with Victoria, the capital, snuggling at the foot of its precipitous slopes. The docks are a mile away, across the harbour on the mainland, at Kowloon. Ships docking have to make a sharp turn to the right to enter their dock, providing a superb view of the island of Hong Kong and the forest of tall buildings in the city across the water. The harbour is always full of ships, mostly anchored and half surrounded with junks and sampans ferrying cargo to and fro. The big square sails of the junks that we saw everywhere have now, alas, almost disappeared, as the junks have become motorized.

The P. and O. agents—Mackinnon and Mackenzie—and the Tourist Organization between them took us everywhere, all over the city, up on to the Peak, across to Aberdeen, the big fishing village where we had a superb meal on a palatial floating restaurant. Then over on the mainland, all through Kowloon and round the so-called New Territories which are on a lease from China for a hundred years, ending in 1997.

I had been asked to convey greetings from the Royal Photographic Society to the Hong Kong photographers. They met us and feted us and took us around, and I gave a lecture to the Photographic Society of Hong Kong. We spent a delightful Sunday morning with the 620 Group, so-called because they invariably catch the first ferry, at 6.20 a.m., across to Kowloon and drive out to the long inlet at Sha-Tin. This is where the beautiful misty effects occur which have made the Hong Kong photographers famous all over the world. It was a perfect morning for this and I tried my luck along with them, using fishing boats and nets with misty mountains in the background. Then I stepped back and photographed this whole group creating their own version of pictorialism with this marvellous material, all eighty of them spread out on a narrow spit of land. One of my pictures was later hung in the London Salon.

I did a lot of industrial photography in Hong Kong, on textiles, ship-building and repairing, aircraft maintenance, food canning, fireworks, thermos flasks, shoes and the famous arts and crafts—ivory and wood carving, cloisonné work and so on. I photographed noodles being made and then hung up on tall racks in the street to dry. We wandered all about the streets, to Cat Street and the well known souvenir centres, always teeming with people, a picture at every corner. We were completely captivated by this quite incredible city.

In Hong Kong I had all our films developed and bought in new supplies. Kodak's were most helpful in every way. I sent all developed films home, with captions, as indeed I had done from India, so that many of our pictures were published long before we got home again. I also wrote a long article about the coach trip to India and this was sent to the *Manchester Guardian* from our office, with a suitable selection of pictures. It was published in two instalments, quite a good display. Later, they published another article on the run from Hong Kong to Japan.

Just before leaving Hong Kong we were asked to go on local television for an interview. There wasn't time, but the P. and O. agents co-operated so that we could do it. We were on the air from 9 p.m. to 9.15 p.m., just an easy going, unrehearsed interview with us as a working team of camera journalists travelling the world. Immediately it was over, we were rushed from the studios by car to Mackinnon Mackenzie's private quay, whisked across to Kowloon on their VIP launch, and so on to the P. and O. cargo ship SUNDA. We sailed at 10 p.m. The other ten passengers had seen us on the ship's television.

We liked the cargo ship, so free from crowds and from the intense organization that always seems to be a part of travelling on a large passenger ship. We were a happy clutch of only twelve passengers; no one seemed to be a misfit, as might so easily happen. We did not proceed directly to Yokohama, but made a two day call at Shanghai, quite a bonus. No visas were required, as we were transit passengers, living on our ship. We tied up in the middle of the broad and always busy Whangpo River. A pleasant young man came on board to tell us about sight-seeing trips that we could take. We went on one lasting several hours which took in most of this great city and finished up with tea and very creamy cakes in a hotel.

On the ship we were warned that no photography whatever was allowed from the vessel, and two armed sentries patrolled the decks continuously. Yet the first place we were taken to on shore was the top of the Shanghai Hotel, at the corner of the Soochow Creek, providing a superb panorama of the whole city, the wharves and the river. Before anyone could say anything, our smiling guide said:

'Yes, you may take photographs from here.'

We looked down at a little bit of Britain in China, a large house in beautiful grounds that was the Shanghai branch of the British Embassy in China, with the Union Jack proudly flying in the gentle breeze. Across the road was a little park, built by the British when they had a concession there. Our guide told us the oft-repeated story of the sign that used to stand at the entrance to it, saying:

'Dogs and Chinese not allowed.'

'Today,' said our guide with a broad grin, 'we even allow British people to go into the park,' and he promptly took us there.

We created a lot of attention in Shanghai, as westerners. We found little groups of people following us, especially when we were shopping. But they were never offensive in any way, and indeed quite bashful when we looked at them and tried to talk. Their dress was dull and uniform, for the most part, generally dark blue trousers and jackets, though the women were breaking out into some colour. The children were a sheer joy, plump and rosy and obviously well fed. In fact, though there were few signs of luxury, there were no signs of abject poverty such as we had seen in India. Food was cheap and plentiful, and everyone seemed to be buying. From the old days of China, before the war and the civil war, this was all hardly recognizable, a vast change for the better. Would it last? I went to China for a much longer trip in 1966, to be described in a later chapter.

We sailed next for Otaru, on Hokkaido, the northernmost of the Japanese islands. It was late winter there, with ice and dirty snow still lingering. We drove up to Sapporo, the capital of the island and quite a large city. It was dominated by a tall radio mast, like the Eiffel Tower in Paris, with observation platforms at various heights. The Japanese had calculated that the outlay on it would be recovered in ten years, from the entrance charges. It had proved so popular that, in less than two years, the whole thing had been paid for.

We spent a month in Japan, right through the cherry blossom season, the early Spring. We covered most of the tourist spots and a good many others besides. We travelled largely by train, and by ship on the beautiful Inland Sea, all among the islands. We went to Nikko on a long one day trip, to see the superb old temples set in a woodland grove, all muted reds and golds, quaint arches and fearsome carved figures guarding the shrines.

The trouble with westerners travelling by train in Japan is that there are few porters and one often has to hump one's own baggage. Furthermore, trains run on such a strict time schedule that, at smaller stations anyway, they depart instantly after their thirty seconds allowance, or whatever it might be, regardless of whether everyone is off or not. Occasionally I found myself flinging the last of our baggage off to Betty on the platform as the train began to move.

The ships on the Inland Sea were ferries of various sizes, with simple but adequate cabins for overnight trips. They were full of uniformed school children who all wanted autographs from every foreigner. They were everywhere, in groups with teachers, quite a feature of the scene wherever we stopped. We went to Kyoto, the old capital, and to Osaka, and the Hakone Park, with magnificent views of Mount Fuji, seen sometimes through the swirling mists erupting from hot mineral springs in the ground.

We stayed at two different Japanese inns, very different from western style hotels. At the front door we took off our shoes and put on sandals. At our bedroom door we shed these and walked about on the springy straw-matted floors in our stockinged feet. We ate in our rooms on low tables, squatting on cushions on the floor. Our beds were normal spring mattresses laid flat on the floor, with no bedsteads. We were given kimonos and were expected to shed our own clothes and go all Japanese.

We walked down the steps into our bath, fed in one hotel by a hot spring from the garden, and we made the unpardonable mistake of not washing and rinsing ourselves first before getting into the bath. Had either of us been travelling alone, we should have probably had a giggling Japanese girl to undress and wash us. The girls in these hotels always seemed to giggle, but it was not meant in any impolite way. It was just an old Japanese custom. Our meals would be cooked at the table, especially such delicacies as sukiyaki, thin slices of beef fried in a delicious sauce, with various vegetables similarly cooked alongside, on a charcoal brazier brought into the room.

At Beppu, in a Japanese Inn, the girl spoke a little English. She asked us if we would like to go into a banquet then being held in a big room in the hotel, and see the entertainment afterwards. We did this, paddling along in our sandals and kimonos, and were warmly welcomed by the two hundred or more Japanese men who had feasted and wined, obviously very well. I took some flash shots of the lovely geisha girls who were handing out little glasses of the famous 'sake' drink, and generally seeing that everyone was being well looked after. Then the president of the banquet took us on the low stage, where dancers had been performing, and made a speech about us, in Japanese. There was much applause and we bowed frequently in Japanese style, from the waist. When we got back to our seats one man who spoke English told us what it was all about. 'This is a convention of plywood dealers,' he explained. 'Our president said that you were customers from England and you were very welcome.'

We went on by train from Beppu to the Aso National Park, where we took a cable car right to the lip of a huge active volcano, where we walked around the precipitous edge dodging the poisonous fumes which swirled up in great clouds. We walked all the way back to our hotel, thousands of feet below, in a cool breeze and warm sunshine, then we returned to Beppu, took an overnight ship to Kobe and boarded the HIMALAYA for India again. But before it sailed the following morning we sallied forth into the city and did our shopping. No country in the world has so much to offer the visitor, not cheap trash but beautiful things of every kind and usually of superb quality.

Early on our third morning out of Kobe, a launch brought the doctor and other officials out to the HIMALAYA as it sailed up the long, island-dotted approach to Hong Kong. I was told to board the launch and thus I was on the dock at Kowloon when the great white ship turned the sharp corner to come in. The weather was perfect. The sun shone brightly, right on to the ship, with the huge dark hill of Hong Kong Island beyond, a perfect setting. I took many pictures as the ship was slowly towed and pushed in by the tugs.

Again, I had all my films developed here. (The shop put on a night shift for me and they got through all our Japanese material.) I was very busy but still found time to do more sight-seeing and to go to parties given by our warm-hearted Chinese photographic friends. We liked Hong Kong.

Two more mornings and I was aroused early as we approached Manila, in the Philippines. This time a dirty old tug put me ashore at the end of a dock, quite deserted and empty. But as I jumped ashore, a man ran out of a shed and, in broken English, said, 'Are you Mr. Cash? Here is your landing permit'.

I got some lovely pictures as the HIMALAYA slowly glided in on a mirror-calm sea in the early morning light. She was a beautiful sight. We had only one day at Manila, but we went out by car to the famous crater and had lunch on the edge, looking down into the lake which now fills the centre. Manila itself is a fine city with modern buildings, old Spanish churches and ancient fortifications all delightfully mixed up.

Three more days at Singapore and one in Colombo, then we were at Bombay again. Now it was the really hot season, with temperatures up to 110°F each day in Delhi. We flew up to Srinagar, the capital of Kashmir, where it was raining and the temperature was only 50°. For four weeks now, in almost perfect weather, we explored this beautiful land, staying most of the time at the Palace Hotel, out of town on the shores of the Dal Lake. It was formerly the home of the Maharajah but was now the leading hotel.

Kashmir in the Spring was sheer bliss. We felt we had earned something of a rest after our long trip, but there was so much to photograph, so much to see, that we were as busy as ever. We took trips away for a few days at a time. We went to Gulmarg, that lovely plateau high above the Vale of Kashmir where the British people used to go in the hot season in the days of the British Raj. Their fine houses were still there but few were occupied and many were decaying.

We went to Sonamarg and rode on horseback high into the mountains, into the snow at over twelve thousand feet and to the edge of great glaciers. This was wild country indeed, not so far from the borders of Tibet. Another trip took us to Pahalgam, in scenery that reminded us of the best of Switzerland. Here, one day, with two Indian students, we went on horseback with guides, across raging streams, through lovely silent pine woods, to come out in a perfect little Alpine meadow, surrounded by huge snow-topped peaks. The river wound across the grassy meadow, dotted with willow trees, and here we let the horses loose and had a day's trout fishing. We caught seven or eight good fish, up to three pounds or so in weight, we had a delightful picnic sitting in the sun, and then we rode back through the woods and the icy streams. The chef at our rest camp made a superb meal for us from our own fish and we invited our two Indian friends to enjoy it with us.

In mid-June we flew back to Bombay, boarded the CARTHAGE and sailed back to England. Through the Suez Canal again, and the Mediterranean, we arrived at London on July 7th, 1959, nine months after leaving home, the longest trip we have ever done, or are ever likely to do, but one of the most exciting and the most productive. There is a lot to be said for travelling by sea.

This was not a cheap trip by any means. We did not get full hospitality everywhere – sometimes only a percentage – and then we extended the trip for a month to include Kashmir, at our own expense. Altogether we estimated that it cost us some £1,700. Quite a lot of money in those days, but all part of the business and a good investment in view of the vast number of photographs we obtained, taken in no less than twenty different countries.

CHAPTER TWELVE

More Commissioned Trips

I suppose that the sensible thing, in the early days of my career, would have been to divide Europe and then the world into countries and regions to be methodically photographed over a number of years, so as not to miss any of them. How dull, how terribly dull! And anyway, how could I have done that? I had no idea then that I would eventually be able to travel anywhere I wanted to, more or less, nor that I would get so much help from so many people and organizations. Such a plan never entered my mind.

The result has been that much of my travelling has been haphazard in the extreme, with many obvious places, islands and countries completely left out. For instance, it was 1972 when I first went to Corsica, and 1966 before I managed to get back to Canada and the U.S.A. Many of my trips come about from invitations, as we have seen. B.E.A. used to send us a list of forthcoming inaugurals early each year, and from these we used to pick out places or countries that would be really useful to us, where we thought we could definitely provide something in return, both to the airline and to the country. But we had to make our choice quickly. B.E.A. could only carry a few journalists on each inaugural, and unless one staked a claim quickly, all the seats would be gone. Sometimes only one of us could go but usually it was both.

In this way we went to Cyprus, Portugal, Prague, Gibraltar, Sardinia, Norway, Turkey, Rhodes and Moscow, among others. In all these, except Moscow, the countries in question offered us hospitality and a conducted tour, either the whole party together, or individually. We found such trips extremely useful and B.E.A. always seemed to be pleased with the publicity we were able to give them. In most cases a set programme was arranged, but not so in the case of Moscow, in 1969. So we went to the Intourist manager in London, told him we had been invited on the inaugural to Moscow and that we would like to take advantage of it by seeing parts of Russia we had not previously visited. Apart from my pre-war trip, I had been back to the Soviet Union with a small party in 1955, and we had both been to Leningrad and Moscow on a school cruise in 1967.

We did a deal with the Intourist manager, whereby we had three weeks in the Soviet Union, in Central Asia, the Caucasus and in Moscow. He asked us to take some 35 mm colour pictures for him, for the automatic projectors which they used for shop window publicity, and a few other special shots, and of course he relied on us publishing some travel articles in due course.

We had a wonderful three weeks, with a guide by the name of Luba, who was most efficient in every way and a delightful person to have with us. Her English was excellent and she really looked after everything so perfectly that we could concentrate completely on our work. We flew down to Tashkent and had a few days in the happy hunting ground of Marco Polo, in Samarkand, Bukhara, Dushanbe, along the Great Silk Road and in much of the country thereabouts. The ancient mosques and fortresses were quite fabulous, most of them now being carefully preserved. We flew on to Tbilisi, in Georgia, and went far and wide by car, through the Caucasus, with a few days on the Black Sea coast. Then back to Moscow and so home. We had no trouble whatever with our cameras, often going out alone, even at night, sometimes taking pictures of night scenes with a tripod, and no one took any more notice than they would do in Britain.

Sometimes we are invited by public relations people to go to some particular country for which they have the account. They know the sort of thing we do, the type of articles we get published and the value of our photographic library. Hence they think we are a good risk, so to speak, and they would like us to do a trip. In this way we have been to Norway several times, to Portugal, Malta more than once and to Jamaica. We had a week in Jamaica with a small press party, followed by a week on our own, with a car and guide, so that we could do a comprehensive coverage of the whole island. From this base we organized a wider coverage to include Barbados, Antigua, Grenada and St. Lucia, a highly successful trip from which we later wrote a number of articles. And of course a very pleasant way of spending part of the winter, with Christmas on Antigua.

We have done two trips to the Bahamas under similar arrangements, one being extended to include Miami. We like the West Indies much more than the Bahamas, though the beaches are as good, the hotels just as plush, and expensive, but the scenery is so much grander altogether in the West Indies, with high mountains, deep valleys and lofty plateaux. Hotel prices in both sets of islands are so fantastic as to be quite frightening. The package tours offered today are, in our opinion, quite incredible bargains.

Apart from our Around Africa trip, one other early invitation came to me in a surprising way. In the post one morning were two stiff printed cards—more cocktail parties, I presumed. The first one was, but the second one read:

'The General Manager of Air Ceylon requests the pleasure of the company of Mr. J. Allan Cash, F.I.B.P., F.R.P.S., on the Ceremonial Opening Flight of Air Ceylon from London to Colombo on 7th February 1956, and on the return flight leaving Colombo on 17th February, and to be the guest of Air Ceylon during the stay on the island.'

Thus began a truly fabulous trip to this lovely tropical island, in the middle of an English winter. It was indeed a ceremonial opening flight, with the entire plane first class, an all-invited passenger list including prominent and titled people from Britain and the Continent, and a few journalists.

I soon discovered how I came to be included in such illustrious company. KLM, the Dutch Airline, were going to operate Air Ceylon, the sort of arrangement often made by smaller countries who want a prestige airline of their own but could not afford to buy planes and absorb all the other vast expenses themselves. The public relations officer of KLM in London had seen much of my material published and made a mental note to include me some time in a trip. This was the time he had chosen. We had never met but we became good friends and it led to other trips with KLM later.

This journey to Ceylon really began with a big dinner party at London Airport, to which Betty was invited. She was talking to General Alers, then President of KLM, who assumed that she was coming on the flight. When she said no, he immediately said:

'Oh, you must. Someone has dropped out and there is a spare seat. Do come with us.'

What a situation for any woman, dressed for a dinner party and with nothing else at all, no baggage, no clothes, nothing! Lady Hoare-Belisha, who was one of the passengers, immediately offered to help Betty out with some of her clothes. But Betty is small and Lady Hoare-Belisha stood nearly six feet tall. It was a minor tragedy but Betty could not come with us.

In Ceylon we were entertained by various prominent people, the climax being an official reception by the Prime Minister at the Government House. There were various trips out to nearby places and around Colombo, all very interesting and to me very glamorous. Michael Barsley, then of the B.B.C., was one of the passengers and he and I soon realized that all the pomp and ceremony was preventing us from doing our work, he recording, me photographing. A quiet word in KLM's ear and hey, presto! We were away up into the mountains with a huge car and a most pleasant guide-chauffeur all to ourselves.

We went up to Kandy and Nuwara Eliya, all among the tea and rubber plantations, staying two nights at Kandy. I thus got hundreds of pictures on countless different subjects in Ceylon. Michael, who had been there before, made up a half hour radio programme from his recordings, which included a brief interview with me standing on the rocks among the crashing waves below the famous Mount Lavinia Hotel outside Colombo. We heard it some weeks later in our own home.

On the morning we left Colombo, Michael and I went down to the Pettah, the big market, and filled huge baskets with every tropical fruit we could find. These delicious products of the tropics lasted us for weeks. The return flight was equally grand, with elaborate meals and all the drinks we could hold. The journey took about thirty hours each way in those days, before jets were used.

In 1960 KLM invited me to go on an inaugural to Turkey, early in January. This is not the best time of the year for Turkey, as the winters are quite cold there, severe indeed inland. But it was a good chance and I received some help from the

Turkish people. I was taken round a lot by car in various parts, usually with the local tourist director.

From Ankara I went out in a coach to see the opening of a big new dam. We got bogged down on muddy roads and missed the opening. But I met a man from the Roads Department of the Government who spoke English. I told him I was going to Görome, that strange place in the centre of Anatolia where pillars of soft rock and the cliffs nearby contain tiny churches and shrines carved into them hundreds of years ago by early Christians. He immediately said he would ask his local representative at Kayseri, where I would have to go by train, to meet me and take me around.

Sure enough, this man met my train and took me to my hotel, right into my room to make sure it was alright. He spoke no English at all but he returned later with an English-speaking student who explained that next day, a Sunday, we would drive to Görome, fifty miles away, and make a day of it. It was a glorious sunny day but bitterly cold, with ice and light snow on some of the roads. The road man could not have been a better host. He took us both to lunch after we had explored all over the strange valley of churches, and then when we returned to Kayseri he insisted on taking us to dinner. I said I must at least pay for this, but he would not hear of it.

I went round the coast on a local ship, from Izmir to Antalya, a beautiful fishing port set in incomparable scenery but sadly lacking in hotels in those days. I had an introduction to the Governor of the province. He spoke excellent English and promptly took me out to lunch. He had just been to England with a small party of Turkish governors to study British civic government, and he was full of praise for the way he and his colleagues had been treated. I received some of the benefits myself. He took me out to see a new irrigation project then under way, then gave me a jeep and driver for several days to go to Alanya and to see some of the quite incredible Roman and Greek remains all along this coast. Huge amphitheatres such as those of Side and Perge, Ephesus and Pergamum, vast ruins that require excavating and preserving, but this is far too big a job for Turkey alone.

Then the Governor told me he was going on a tour of the province for a few days and would I like to accompany him. I certainly would. We set off early one morning, in a big Mercedes car, complete with chauffeur and a young German student, a nice chap. At every village and town we came to a small crowd of men were waiting for the Governor. He would get out to greet them, then the whole group would assemble in some café or school room, where he heard their complaints and issued orders to have them remedied. He always asked me to sit beside him and told me briefly what was being said. In one village, Akçay, the sun shone strong and warm, so the meeting was held on the pavement outside, with dozens of chairs dragged out from various cafes. I excused myself after a short time, so that I could photograph the scene.

Here we left our big car and got into two jeeps, to go for hours over a big range of mountains, clothed with giant cedars which must have been identical, I think, with the cedars of Lebanon, now almost extinct in the Lebanon Mountains. For hours we bumped along on a rough trail, with no villages or any form of human dwelling. Then, at dusk, we dropped down a long series of hairpin bends to the tiny fishing village of Demre, called Myra in ancient times. This, I discovered, was where Santa Claus originated, in the form of Bishop Nicholas, of Myra, famous for giving presents to people far and wide. His little church was there, now restored but mostly underground, and his tomb was nearby. But his body was removed to Brindisi many centuries ago, as it was not thought to be safe in a Moslem land.

We sailed across the bay in a fishing boat next morning, having spent the night in various private homes, after a big feast given by the mayor in one of the houses. The Governor was to see a new road being built along the coast to Demre. As we scrambled ashore and climbed up on to the site, a man slew a sheep in front of our eyes and scattered the blood over the road. For good luck, I presume. Then, after the inspection, we sat down on wooden packing cases and were served with freshly cooked fish caught that morning, while the rock drills and bulldozers roared away close by. As we sailed back across the bay, camels were coming down through the sand dunes groaning under crates of locally grown oranges, to be loaded on to a small sailing ship.

The next year, 1961, KLM put a proposition to me, whereby they would buy a number of my existing pictures outright, where I could spare the negatives, at quite a good price. But they would pay me with a credit to travel on their airline, to wherever I wanted to go, in order to take more photographs. They insisted that this must be first class air travel, as I would, in effect, be working for them. This was an arrangement approved of by I.A.T.A. but it could not include Betty. I had the exquisite pleasure of poring over KLM's route maps covering the whole world, deciding where I would like to go. I finally decided on South America, as I had not been anywhere there so far.

Thus one evening I left London Airport in a big KLM plane for the long flight to Rio de Janeiro, the beginning of a three months' trip through parts of Brazil, Uruguay, Argentina and Chile. I received little help from any of these countries as they did not at that time have any budget to help journalists. So I had to do my best with some minor hotel concessions, and reductions on certain internal airlines. It was an expensive trip but one I never regret having made. It enhanced our library enormously.

Before I left home I went to see Sir Derek Vestey, whose company have big interests in the meat industry of Brazil and the Argentine. He gave me introductions which resulted in my staying on two of their big fazendas (ranches) in the interior of Brazil, where I photographed cattle being fattened up for the big frigorificos run by the company. One fazenda covered more than sixty thousand acres and I was driven over many parts of it by the manager. In both fazendas I stayed in the managers' bungalows. I also photographed the whole process of meat production again in Buenos Aires later on, from the cattle and sheep arriving at the stockyards, to their slaughter (quite humane and quick) and the cutting up and freezing of the meat. This is one long continuous process right into the huge freezing chambers where the meat, still warm, caused a dense fog that I found a nuisance. I also shot frozen carcases being loaded on to a Blue Star liner in the docks, a shipping line owned by the same Vestey interests.

In Rio I stayed at a hotel right on the famous Copacabana Beach. At Sao Paulo I booked a room high up in a hotel in order to get pictures by night as well as day of this quite incredible city, still I believe the fastest growing town in the world. Rio is very beautiful, set on a vast bay, with strangely shaped mountains all round. It is huge and crowded and noisy, with some appalling slums, not quite as glamorous as many people believe. Sao Paulo is pure business, often big business, and has one of the worst traffic problems in the world.

I could not be in Brazil without seeing Brasilia, the new capital, built right out in the open spaces far away inland. It has some really magnificent architecture and some beautiful aspects. But why, oh why, is not a new city built from the centre outwards, so that it is not always a case of great open spaces in the middle and all the buildings so far apart that travelling about in the city assumes nightmarish qualities?

Montevideo was, by contrast, a quiet and compact city, not too large as yet. I went inland with a foreign agricultural expert from the United Nations, to visit numerous farms and inspect crops. Uruguay is a green and pleasant land, often quite pretty, with a pleasant climate, lacking the fierce heat of the great Brazilian plains.

Buenos Aires, further up the vast estuary of the River Plate, is a huge sprawl of a city. From here again I was taken out to farms on the vast flat pampas, and would gladly have seen more of these endless grassy plains. I went to the big seaside resort Mar del Plata, with the largest casino in the world, and lovely big sandy beaches. Then I flew over the Andes to Santiago de Chile, to come back to the Argentine later on.

Santiago is a pleasant smallish city, standing at the foot of the Andes, near to Aconcagua, the highest peak, which is over twenty two thousand feet above sea level. I had a commission to take some photographs of the really high Andes for a firm in England, but they had to be taken from high, not from below looking up. The only road over the Andes, a hundred miles away, was blocked with snow, so I solved the problem by hiring a small plane and flying alongside the vast range at sixteen thousand feet. The pilot spoke no English but before taking off we had arranged certain signals, so we had no problems. Only the lack of oxygen at that height bothered me. It was too sudden a rise and I was glad to get down again, to breathe normally.

I went down to Valparaiso, a lovely city and port on the coast, then I started on a long and complicated trip southwards. First I travelled by train to Concepcion and took a lot of photographs in the big steelworks. A kindly professor at the University sent me out in his car to a wild spot on the coast and through the surrounding countryside. Then I continued by train right down as far as the railway goes, to Puerto Montt. This is also the southern limit of the Pan American

Highway. Beyond here, down to Punta Arenas and Cape Horn, the coast is so rugged and broken that no road could possibly be built.

From Puerto Varas, close by, I set off after a few days on a wonderful journey through the Andes to Bariloche, in Argentina. First I went inland by bus, then transferred to a small steamer which took me along a lake between huge snow-covered mountains, with glaciers gleaming on their slopes. Then another bus and another ship on a lake and so on, right into the Lake Huapi National Park in the Argentine, with a stop overnight at a small hotel about half way. The scenery on this route is magnificent, with the great mountains, clear cool lakes, raging rivers and waterfalls and the most beautiful forests, full of berberis and other flowering bushes under the great trees. Bariloche looks just like an Austrian mountain town and was, indeed, set up by Austrian emigrants. I had several delightful days there, climbing mountains and going out on the big lake. Then back to Buenos Aires for a few days and home again by KLM. A wonderful journey altogether. South America was a good choice.

In 1955 we realized that we had not yet been to Norway. I went round to the Norwegian Embassy in London one autumn day to see what could be done about it. I met a Mr. Lemkuhl, a sort of Minister-at-Large for Norway, a charming elderly diplomat known affectionately by one and all as 'Excellency'. He heard my story, looked at my cuttings and then said:

'Mr. Cash, will you go round right away to the Bergen Line offices in Cockspur Street and ask for Mr. Stanley, the managing director. I will telephone and tell him you are on your way.'

Surprised and puzzled, I did as he asked. Mr. Stanley was accompanied by John O'Dell, his publicity manager. They listened politely to my story, looked at my cuttings, then a knowing look passed between them and Mr. Stanley said:

'Before the war we used to organize a winter sports contest in Norway between British and Norwegian universities. We are going to revive this idea next March and we are looking for a photographer to cover the event. Could you do it?'

I assured him that I could. I had been looking for a trip to Norway the following summer but why not tackle it in winter and get something of Norwegian winter sports? We agreed that Betty and I would leave ten days early and see something of Voss, Vatnerhalsen and Finse before going on to Geilo, where the universities' events would take place. All these places are on the famous Bergen—Oslo Railway, one of the most remarkable in the world. We did a story on that as well. The Norwegian Tourist Organization co-operated and so began the long and pleasant relationship we have enjoyed with Norway and the Bergen Line to this day. We produced the sort of pictures they required on the first occasion, so we have been invited back time after time.

We returned the next summer, with our car, and did a long motoring trip through the fjord country, surely just about the most exciting and rewarding motoring in Europe, as long as you are not in a hurry and have a good head for heights. Then we left the car at Bergen and sailed on a two weeks' cruise on the

Bergen Line luxury ship METEOR, up to the North Cape and all in among the fjords and the Lofoten Islands.

We have been back to Norway a number of times, again driving our car across to Oslo and back, and we have done the twelve day coastal trip several times. This is the daily service of steamers, operated jointly by five companies, which run all the way from Bergen round the North Cape to Kirkenes, near the Soviet border, and back again, calling at some sixty ports on the way. In the summer season these ships carry a limited number of tourists, with some well organized and quite ambitious shore excursions. We think it is one of the best trips anywhere in Europe, from every point of view.

More recently we went on what is known as the Express Route, a variation of the same theme. The ships stop at fewer places up to the North Cape, then strike off into the Arctic to Spitzbergen, again with shore excursions on these strange islands half covered with snow and glaciers. From the northern part of the main island we sailed up to the edge of the Polar Ice, a thrilling experience. The most remarkable feature of these cold Arctic waters is the vast number of sea birds to be seen everywhere, flying about in huge flocks—puffins, razorbills, guillemots, auks and gulls, to mention only a few. I wrote an article for *Country Life* on this subject after our return.

Another icy trip I did one March, this time with a doctor friend, was to the Lofoten Islands, to do a story on the cod fishing industry. Early each year, great numbers of Arctic cod come down to breed in the wide expanses of the Vestfjord, the sea between the Lofotens and the mainland of Norway. Fishing boats gather in the Lofoten ports to catch them, up to five thousand vessels at a time. Only lines are permitted and fishing can only be done in daylight hours. Bergen Line asked us to make a cine record of this remarkable event.

We went up from Bergen on the normal coastal service and made our headquarters at Svolvaer. Every day there were blinding blizzards of snow—the snow was late that year—but brilliant sunshine in between. And every day we went out with our cameras. We got some beautiful effects, in cine as well as stills, of hundreds of boats sailing out of Henningsvaer at dawn, against the sunrise, with their lights still on. We went out on small ships among the fishing fleets and got dramatic pictures of them, with a backdrop of the dazzling white ramparts of the great Lofoten Wall. And we fished ourselves and caught cod by our own efforts.

We covered the whole process of the cod being landed, gutted and processed, even of the school children cutting out the tongues from the discarded cods' heads. They are considered a great delicacy and the children sell them from door to door. John O'Dell made an excellent little film out of our cine material, cutting, editing and doing the commentary all himself. He called it 'Fish and Ships'.

Our friendly connection with Bergen Line has resulted not only in various trips to Norway, but to Madeira and the Canary Islands as well. Madeira is one of our favourite islands, with its wild and dramatic mountains, its colourful little fishing villages, and the quaint and so distinctly Portuguese capital of Funchal. The last time we went, 1971, was for the opening of the big new Hilton Hotel. The same year we were in Norway for the opening of the SAS Royal Hotel at Bodo, fifty miles north of the Arctic Circle. A big luxury hotel in a small fishing town, far up in the north, but apparently fully justified. It seems to be full throughout the year, with tourists and conventions.

CHAPTER THIRTEEN

China

My trip to China really began in Jamaica! Betty and I, with the small press party, were being entertained to lunch at the Round Hill Hotel by James Duncan and his wife. He was a famous Canadian industrialist, having been president of the Massey Harris Company until he retired early, then Chairman of the Ontario Hydro-electric Commission. During the lunch he told me that, five years previously, he had been invited to visit China, by the Chinese Government, to see what they were doing industrially under communism. He had gone, with his wife, a most charming Spanish lady, and he had been much impressed with what he saw. He had written some articles in the Toronto press describing his observations, ending up by saying that, in spite of much progress, he still thought capitalism was a better system.

To his surprise he had just received another invitation, to revisit China the following year, and he proposed to go.

'You ought to take a photographer with you next time,' I exclaimed, 'and do it properly'.

I meant it as a joke but he took me seriously.

'Would you really like to go to China?' he asked.

'I can think of no country I would rather visit than China.'

He said he would write to his contacts in China and suggest that I be invited as well. I thought no more of it. But months later I suddenly received a telephone call from the Chinese Charge d'Affaires' office in London asking me to go down to see them. I went and was asked a lot of questions about myself, my work, my political leanings if any, and so on, all to the accompaniment of innumerable cups of green tea. No mention whatever was made about my possibly visiting China, and I duly departed, back to my office.

Weeks later I received a similar call, and this time we got down to it. Many more questions. Many more cups of green tea. All in an atmosphere of extreme cordiality. I was told that I could go to China with Mr. Duncan, leaving Hong Kong on September 1st. This was 1964, before the Cultural Revolution. We had to find our own way to Hong Kong. It was not possible for Betty to go with me this time.

I flew direct to Hong Kong, having decided not to stop off anywhere but to make use of being so far from home on the way back. China came first. I met Mr.

and Mrs. Duncan late in August, renewed acquaintance with the Hong Kong photographers, gave them a lecture and completed my arrangements for six weeks in China. I also took many photographs of Hong Kong, though it was terribly hot and sticky.

We left by train from Kowloon for the Chinese border, crossed the famous bridge from the New Territories and we were in China. There was a long but most comfortable wait in a luxurious waiting room, our passports were taken away by polite officials, and duly returned, then an excellent lunch was served and we were on a train for Canton. We had been invited by the Chinese Council for the Promotion of International Trade, a very important body. Their representative met us at Canton and took us to our hotel, quite a good one but rather far out. From now on we had with us a woman interpreter (for the Duncans), a young man as my interpreter, and another man who spoke no English but who was some sort of political commissar. Every question we asked was referred to him and he gave the answer. It was all rather tedious and time consuming but that was the system.

Everywhere in China we were a great curiosity to the Chinese people. They stared at us and they often followed us about in little groups. But they were never aggressive. Whenever I changed a film in the street or any public place, I would hear little shufflings and whispering behind me. I took no notice but when I was ready I would suddenly swing my camera round on to a little crowd of people and there would be mock cries of alarm and panic. It is considered most impolite to photograph anyone in China without first asking their permission. Whenever I did ask, and language was no barrier, everyone wanted to be in the picture. I soon learnt to like the Chinese. They are so polite and friendly.

We were taken all round Canton and out into the country, then we flew up to Peking, in a British Viscount plane bought by the Chinese. Now they use British Tridents. In Peking we met our hosts and were entertained to a fabulous banquet. Our main contact turned out to be a Mr. Hou Ton who had spent sixteen years in England with the Bank of China, latterly as manager in London, until about 1960. He was now a leading financial adviser, really a cabinet minister, often sent abroad to conferences by the government.

We all took part in a long conference to decide our itinerary. Then, on a Sunday, Mr. Hou Ton and his wife and daughter, took us out to the Great Wall and to the Ming Tombs, with an out-door picnic lunch. We talked of England, of London and Hampstead, where the Hou Ton's had lived. I told them of the nice new flat, complete with our own garden, that Betty and I had moved to in Hampstead, and they knew just where it was. It was all very pleasant and a beautiful sunny day.

Most of the time I travelled with the Duncans, but we parted company occasionally for a day or two, with different programmes, and came together again later. They could only spare five weeks; I was asked to stay the full six weeks. We spent a few days in Peking, an enormously wide-spread city, then went to Chungking by train, some fifteen hundred miles away, with stops at Loyang and Sian. Now we were really seeing China, with visits to factories, communes and so on. It was all completely fascinating to me; I could write a book on this trip alone. But I will concentrate on the photographic aspects.

There were no restrictions at all on my photography, except that I was asked not to take any pictures from the air. Otherwise, in factories, communes, schools, in the streets and the parks, wherever I went I could take pictures. I went through a big tractor factory in Loyang, a steelworks at Wuhan and other factories elsewhere. In all of them I was asked if there was anything they could do to help me to get my photographs. People were moved about and posed, machinery was stopped or started, corners were tidied up. I could not have been better treated.

Nearly everywhere we went, the local itinerary included a tour of the nearby countryside, a visit to a commune or two. I enjoyed this enormously and built up quite a number of pictures on communes, so that I was able to write long articles about them when I returned home. We spent a few days in Shanghai, and went on by train to Hangchow, that exquisitely beautiful resort in the hills to the south, with temples and lakes and islands and goldfish ponds and everything that is traditionally Chinese. We walked on a bridge on The Island of Three Ponds that Mirror the Moon. We fed the hundreds of fish in Hua Chang's Goldfish Pond, and we went into The Pagoda of the Six Harmonies.

Then we flew back to Peking in time for the October 1st celebrations, with the huge parade in the morning and the fireworks and dancing after dark. I have never seen anything like it. We had seats on the stands beneath the great gate to the Forbidden City, the Tien an Men, with Mao Tse Tung, Chou en Lai and all the other leaders above us. Promptly at ten o' clock the parade began along the enormously wide street. It was all sheer uninhibited colour, not a military parade at all. There were huge floats, masses of people dressed in costumes, waving huge red flags; sometimes they marched two hundred abreast along the street. At precisely midday the last of them marched past us. In those two hours half a million people had passed in that gigantic parade. The enormous square beyond, rightly called the Great Square, held a million more, all in formation. They held bouquets of some material in various colours, and above the heads of the marchers great slogans would flash across the dense crowd as they held up their colours in a variety of precise patterns. Not a single spot of colour in all that mass was ever out of place.

The next evening we attended a huge banquet for all the six thousand foreign visitors, held in the Great Hall of the People. Another night a great pageant called 'The East is Red' was held in the largest theatre in the same great building, with fifteen hundred people on the stage and a choir of another fifteen hundred at the sides. Duncan was not very impressed with it, but I thought it was magnificent, by any standards.

An old friend of ours, Dr. Jos Horne, was living in Peking at this time and I spent many pleasant hours with him and his wife and family at their Chinese home. Some ten years earlier he had been asked to go out to China to teach surgery, on a four year contract. He had been so intrigued with all that was going on in China that he had twice more renewed his contract and returned after leave at home. He told me much about the medical services in China and of his own particular work. It was at his hospital that the famous case occurred of the factory worker's hand that was torn off in a machine and replaced by surgery, completely successfully. He and his Chinese colleagues were doing many interesting things in medicine, and the government had built a special hospital for them, specializing in accidents and burns. Their work has been written up in British medical journals.

His wife was teaching and both their children had been educated at Chinese schools. The boy was then at Peking University, apparently a brilliant student in electronics even by Chinese standards. Later on, both of them took an active part in the Cultural Revolution, spending many months in remote villages educating the peasants and helping them with their work. They are all now back in this country and it is interesting to talk to them. They give a very different account of recent events in China than most of us have learnt from reading our own papers.

The Duncans left China after the ceremonies but Hou Ton arranged for me to go to Manchuria, now known as North-East China. My interpreter came with me, and now it seemed I did not need the commissar. We two got on well together. His English was excellent and he arranged visits to factories, coal mines and communes. I went to the great steelworks at Anshan and took many photographs inside, of blast furnaces, rolling mills and steel furnaces. There were no restrictions whatever. We went on to Fushun, to see the enormous open cast coalmine, a hole in the ground five miles long, a mile wide and hundreds of feet deep.

We went to a retired miners' home, a propaganda place if you like, but a very good one and I believe there are many more like it. I talked to some of the old miners and they all lined up for photographs. They were certainly happy in their old age. Then I went to a nearby medical spa and saw some extraordinary cures going on, including the ancient art of cupping brought up to date. My hosts insisted on my taking a bath and having a short sleep. It was the biggest bath I have ever been in. I positively floated in it. But I felt extremely relaxed and refreshed afterwards, thanks presumably to the mineral salts in the water.

It was getting bitterly cold so far north, and indeed it was late autumn. I flew down to Peking for one last night, where I was banqueted again, then on to Canton alone and was met there for a final day's tour around the city. Here it was hot but not so humid as when we arrived. Then came the three hour train journey to the border and so back to Hong Kong. One of the officials on the station recognized me, asked me what I thought of China and when I started to open my bags for examination, he exclaimed:

'Oh, no, Mr. Cash. You are our guest. We do not want to look inside your bags. Come back again some day.'

And so I left China, with all my films undeveloped, my bags still locked. I had been invited as a photographer and so there were no restrictions imposed on me whatever. Could I ask for more?

I had all my films developed in Hong Kong, as before, and bought more film from Kodak. Then I spent ten days photographing everything, all over Hong Kong Island and the New Territories. I booked to go to Macau for a couple of days, but a typhoon blew up and I never got there. A typhoon in the China Sea is an extraordinary experience. Winds of a hundred miles an hour can do incredible things, especially when, as this time, they are accompanied by thirteen inches of rain in less than twenty-four hours. Even so, I managed to take a few photographs at the height of the storm, well sheltered from the shop signs and sheets of metal that were flying through the air horizontally, like leaves off trees.

I flew on to Bangkok and had three days there, my first visit to Thailand. What an incredible mixture of rather shabby modern with the most exquisite temples of unbelievable beauty and colour. I went out into the country with two young men from T.O.T., the tourist organization. The countryside was extremely beautiful, with level patches of intensely green rice paddies and groups of trees. Boys rode bareback on buffaloes and women in wide straw hats fished in little ditches. We went to Nakorn Pathom, with its huge golden temple, the Phra Pathom Chedi, and ancient royal palaces. I must see more of Thailand one of these days.

Then I flew to Beirut to meet Betty. We had three weeks as the guests of the Lebanon and Jordan Tourist Organizations, in the golden autumn of the Middle East, three weeks during which we climbed high up in to the Lebanon Mountains, explored Beirut and the old city of Jerusalem, then in Jordan. We bathed in the warm waters of the Gulf of Aqaba, and rode on horseback into the ancient Nabattean city of Petra. The weather was warm and dry, just perfect, and we enjoyed every minute of it. Then we flew home and I began the long job of sorting out all my Chinese material, making up sets of pictures and writing articles. The *Illustrated London News* published many of my pictures over three issues. I wrote articles on communes, railways, steel, photography, children, tourism, medical services and various other subjects. My pictures have been in great demand; China was one of my most successful trips, with Hong Kong, Thailand, Lebanon and Jordan as bonuses.

CHAPTER FOURTEEN

North America

Perhaps the most strenuous trip we have ever done was to North America. We badly needed to photograph the U.S.A., so one day late in 1965, we went to see Bev Miller, the United States Travel Manager in London. We had known him for a long time and he was always asking us when we were going to America. Now we told him we were ready to go.

'Why don't you go to Canada and Mexico at the same time?' he asked. He told us that these three countries had a combined scheme whereby they invited a limited number of journalists each year to visit their countries, all in one trip. It had to be for a minimum of three weeks, equally divided between the three. Time was not the most important factor; it was up to the journalists as to how long they could spare. We were not tied down for time so we could make a good plan. We eventually worked out a seven weeks' trip, with sixteen days in each country. I planned an itinerary, submitted it through Bev to the three countries, who made only minor changes, and it was fixed.

Bev said it was a killer of a trip, even by American standards. It meant moving on every other day, on an average, for seven weeks, without a week-end or a day off anywhere, shooting all the time. Bev assured us that we would be met and shown round everywhere, all hotels would be booked, and every air flight would be confirmed. We need do none of this ourselves. If this was really so, then the plan was possible. If anything went wrong we would soon be in serious trouble. We could not alter the itinerary in any way, for obvious reasons.

We were to start in New York on May 3rd., then go on to Washington, Chicago and New Orleans. After that we would do Mexico and return to the States sixteen days later to cover Denver, Salt Lake City, the Grand Canyon, Las Vegas, San Francisco and Seattle. From there we would go by ferry to Victoria, British Columbia, by ferry again from Nanaimo to Vancouver and by train to Jasper. After a couple of days in this glorious national park we were to go by coach to Lake Louise and Banff, then by train to Calgary. We would fly to Toronto, Ottawa and Quebec and finish up at Montreal. Most of our travelling would be by air, some twenty thousand miles and it would all be first class. The hotels would be top class—Hiltons and the equivalent wherever possible.

Hotels and meals were financed in a special way in these three countries. Instead of each hotel sending in an account to cover our stay afterwards, we were given so many dollars per day and we paid our own expenses. The amount was not sufficient to cover everything, but many of the hotels—most in fact—gave us special rates, some even making no charge at all for our room. Thus the allowance was enough and we were not out of pocket. I kept a careful account of all our expenses and we just about broke even. For extra expenses such as taxis, airport coaches and so on, we were reimbursed on our return home. Could we ask for more?

Two weeks before we were due to start I received an invitation from Air Canada to go on an inaugural flight from London to Vancouver, non-stop, with a group of other journalists. It would leave just one week before our big trip began. I said yes, immediately visualizing an extra week in Canada. Given the facilities, I would not return to London after the four days with the rest of the journalists but would remain in Canada, drifting back to Toronto and flying down to New York to meet Betty when she arrived. This worked perfectly.

It was a tremendous thrill to me to be back in Canada after so many years. I always loved Vancouver and found it even more entrancing than I remembered. When the others departed, I went by train on the Canadian Pacific through the Rockies to Calgary. I felt elated, having done this journey more than once when I was living in Canada. Calgary was covered by a late snowfall, so I got winter pictures. Six weeks later, when Betty and I arrived in Calgary, it was hot and sunny so then we took summer pictures.

I arrived in New York an hour before Betty came in from London. She has cousins in New York but we had never met them. She wrote to tell them of our plans and they promised to meet us. Incredibly, they found me among the seething crowds at Kennedy Airport and we waited together. I was able to introduce Betty to her own cousins! They are delightful people and we all got on like a house of fire, from the word go. They took us everywhere in New York. We have seen them again since, and they have visited us in England. It is always a particular pleasure to be with them.

This was the first time I had been in New York since 1936. What an incredible place it is—exciting, noisy, crowded, yet often really beautiful in its own peculiar way. Betty's cousin had an office on Fifth Avenue, high above New York Public Library, with what I think must be one of the finest views anywhere in Manhattan. I made good use of it, by night as well as day. We went everywhere and did all the usual things, photographing all the time. One day we were in a taxi on our way to luncheon with an English journalist we knew from London. Betty was telling her about our travels but when she paused for a moment, the taxi driver said:

'Lady, keep right on talking. I can believe I am listening to an English film star.'

I always thought Betty had a good voice. When we left the taxi, the driver turned to Betty and said:

'Lady, you've made my day.'

New York taxi drivers are an entertainment in themselves.

We had incredibly good luck with the weather on this ambitious trip. It was raining in Chicago when we arrived but it cleared immediately and we had three days of brilliant sunshine. It had been raining for a week in Washington but was perfect for our three days there. When we left it was raining again. Only in Seattle did we not see the sun at all. Bad weather could have been disastrous, as we had no spare time anywhere. It was sunny at Denver and Salt Lake City. We gazed down into the Grand Canyon in brilliant moonlight on the night we arrived there. I don't remember any rain in Mexico or Canada.

We wasted the minimum amount of daylight hours travelling. Many of our flights took place first thing in the morning, so that we were on the job in a new city by mid-morning. Others were in the evenings so that, in some cases, we had dinner on the plane and could go straight to our hotel, have a good night's rest and be ready to start early next morning. Only the long flight from Mexico City to Denver took a good part of the day, but even then we were on the job as soon as we arrived. On this part of the trip we moved on every day, so good arrangements and good weather were absolutely essential.

I realized before we ever left home that, whatever happened, we must avoid getting over-tired, with such a tight programme. Hence we sometimes declined invitations to visit night clubs and theatres. Our hosts were very understanding. Often enough we ordered dinner in our room—what excellent service one gets in this way in American, Canadian and many Mexican hotels—and so we did not even have to change but could relax completely. Only in Las Vegas did we break this rule, and how could we do otherwise in this f:ntastic desert city of gamblers?

We were met at Las Vegas airport in the early evening, whisked straight into the dining-room-cum-theatre in our hotel, to have dinner with our hosts while we watched the most elaborate and colourful stage show imaginable. Then they drove us down to the Golden Mile, still with the dust of the Grand Canyon on our shoes, where we were soon taking snapshots in the streets in the unbelievably brilliant lighting, all from signs and shop windows. I don't think they bother with street lights in Las Vegas. None of the shops or gambling saloons ever close. Many of them do not even have doors that could be locked. Everything goes on forever, throughout the year.

Mexico was everything we had hoped for. A beautiful mountainous country, with countless magnificent pyramids and ruined temples—there are more than eleven thousand archaeological sites in the country—tropical beaches, beautiful old Spanish cities like Taxco, Guernavaca and Oaxaca and the vast jungles of the Yucatan, in the south. We liked the Yucatan best of all with its ancient cities and huge pyramids, only comparatively recently rescued from the smothering embrace of the jungle trees and creepers. I think the sight of Chichenitsa, its great white buildings gleaming in the sunlight, spread over a wide area of open grassland now, with the jungle pushed well back, is one of the most exciting archaeological sites I have ever seen. But then Uxmal, Mitla, Monte Alban and Teotihuacan, each unique and different, are really just as dramatic in their own way. Right in the heart of Mexico City itself, during excavations for a vast building site only a few years ago, ruins of the original Aztec capital of Tenochtitan, then on an island in a lake, were unearthed. The Mexicans think so highly of their archaeological sites that they immediately altered the plans for the big housing estate to save the ruins. These now occupy a newly created park in the midst of the tall blocks of flats.

Mexico City was bigger than we had expected (population over five million) and far too noisy and crowded for comfort. But it is over seven thousand feet above sea level and has a splendid climate. We spent a few days there, then drove down to Acapulco by road, spending a night at Taxco, the silver city, on the way. From the Pacific coast we flew to Oaxaca, then back to the capital and on to Merida, in the Yucatan. From each centre we were driven far out into the country, to the famous sites, to silver mines, old towns and villages and monasteries, to the floating gardens of Xochimilco and to some of the most colourful markets we have ever seen. We would like to return and see much more of Mexico.

I thought Betty might be disappointed in Canada, as I had said so much about it over many years. Possibly I had oversold it. But she fell for it as hard as I did years ago when I went to live there. She particularly liked Montreal, one of the most beautiful and exciting cities in the world today, with some really inspired developments and complexes of buildings. I was thrilled to notice the changes since the 1930's when I had last seen it. I still think that the view down from Mount Royal, the hill in the middle of the city, is one of the best of any town anywhere, with the St. Lawrence River beyond the cluster of tall buildings. But let us begin in the West.

Our train to Jasper started from Vancouver in the afternoon, so we saw much of the Fraser Canyon and beyond in daylight. The night was clear and moonlit and Betty sat up in her bunk most of the night, spellbound by the wild gorges, the rushing torrents and lofty peaks of the Rockies. Jasper Park Lodge, with its wooden chalets scattered along the lake shore was sheer delight. We just relaxed and lapped it all up.

When I lived in Canada, there was no road between Jasper and Banff. Today there is a first class highway and a most scenic one. We rode out on to the Columbia Icefield on a snowcat, where previously hardy skiers could only get there after days of hard toil. Lake Louise, a green-blue gem beneath hanging glaciers, was as beautiful as ever, and bears came out on to the road to be fed from passing cars, a risky business if you value your fingers.

After Calgary we had a slight let-up, the only break in our tight programme. Steve Anderson, the P.R.O. of Air Canada had arranged for us to stay privately on the ranch of a former commodore of the airline, Howard Sandgathe. He said we would all get on well together. We had to go on the Canadian Pacific trans-Continental express from Calgary to Brook, a flag stop a hundred miles to the east. The Sandgathes were to meet us there. Would they be there, we wondered? The half-mile long train duly stopped at the tiny station and there were two people who could only be our hosts. We all took to each other instantly.

They drove us fifty miles to their ranch, where they bred beef cattle over twenty five thousand acres. Their lovely house, for all its isolation, was fully modernized, complete with deep freeze, an all electric kitchen and everything that even a city could provide. We had four marvellous days there, photographing all the time. We drove far and wide over the vast plains. We saw cattle branding on another ranch, and we went down to the banks of the Red Deer River, on their estate, and collected fossils of dinosaur bones and other strange animals that roamed the district a hundred and fifty million years ago. Just across the river was the Alberta Dinosaur Park, where complete skeletons have been found. We were really sorry to leave our new friends, but eventually they drove us to Calgary where we caught an Air Canada plane for Toronto.

Then followed strenuous days in eastern Canada and so finally home, appropriately on a B.O.A.C. VC10 plane. The only effect we noticed after this highly organized trip was that it was a little harder to get up for the first few mornings at home. Otherwise we did not seem to have suffered in any way at all. We came home with a rich bag of new pictures, and soon we were writing articles on various aspects of our experiences. It was a good trip altogether.

CHAPTER FIFTEEN

Australia and Around the World

In all our travels to date, we have only once been round the world, mostly because there was no point in it. It is always particular countries and places we are interested in, not making patterns round the earth. But when we went to Australia, in 1967, there was a point to it. It is just about the same distance from Sydney to London either way, so having gone out eastwards, we continued in the same general direction.

We had a newly married nephew in Melbourne taking his Ph.D. at Monash University, so one day I said to Betty:

'Let's go to Australia while Michael and Hazel are still there.'

It seemed to me to be as good an excuse as any other to visit the Antipodes. We knew the Australian tourist director in London and he had said more than once that he wanted us to visit his country. We went to see him one day and said we were now ready. He was delighted and in no time at all we were poring over maps in his office and deciding where we should go. His organization made it a rule that they could not help journalists to get to Australia. It was more than their budget could stand. So we had to make our own arrangements.

'Let's go and see Qantas,' I suggested. 'Always fly by the air line of the country you are going to.'

We don't always do this but it seemed a good idea. We went straight round to Qantas, all three of us. The publicity manager in London knew of us, though we had not met so far. He listened to our plans, then said:

'This is splendid. Let us see what we can arrange.'

We discussed dates and flights and then he said:

'Mr. and Mrs. Cash, let me say right away that I am on your side. I want you to go to Australia and I want you to fly Qantas.'

Sometimes we have to battle with airlines to convince them that it will be worth their while to co-operate. This was a pleasant change. We found there was an inaugural flight taking place on September 28th to Sydney. It was just the time we wanted to go, so he put the proposition to his head office. He wasn't sure if they would agree to take us both on this flight. But they did, quite quickly, so our transport was laid on. We said we would go on round the world. It is slightly further across the Pacific and we had to pay the difference. Not too serious.

The office of the New Zealand Travel Commissioner in London, Mr. Bern, was our next port of call. We told him we would like to visit his country after Australia and again, right away, we were looking at maps and planning our itinerary. New Zealand is a small country and they offered us a perfectly marvellous tour through both islands at a very much reduced rate, all in. They could not afford full hospitality for journalists at that time. We accepted at once, of course, and then went to see the company that does publicity for Fiji. Here again we were well enough known for the answer to be immediately 'yes'. We worked out a two weeks' trip in Fiji.

We had the alternative of two Qantas routes home, either Tahiti and Mexico, or Hawaii and the U.S.A. We chose the latter. Here the usual American plan for journalists of so much per day came in, with some hotels offering us concessions as well, so that the amount we received covered most normal expenses. We were to spend ten days in the Hawaiian Islands, including Christmas. That should be fun, we thought.

An old friend of ours, John Lloyd, was Consul-General at Osaka at that time and he was home on leave with his wife. We told them of our plans, which included a stop-over at San Francisco.

'I am being posted there,' he exclaimed. 'Cancel your hotel and stay with us.'

And so we did, eventually, over the New Year. Then to New York for a few days to see those truly delightful and warm-hearted cousins of Betty's and to stay at our favourite hotel, the Berkshire. We would arrive home again early in January.

It is a long way to Sydney. We would have liked to break the journey at least once but, being on an inaugural, we had to go the whole distance on the one plane. Returning, whichever way we travelled, we could stop off as often as we wanted. We survived. It was a twenty-nine hour journey, too long and we were tired, but fortunately time lag never bothers us, as it does so many people. Give us one good night's sleep after our arrival anywhere and we are normal again. We are lucky in this respect.

We had six weeks in Australia, first in and around Sydney, then a three days' coach tour of the Snowy Mountains, with their superb scenery and quite incredible hydro-electric scheme. Whole rivers are turned round, pushed through tunnels often miles long, and made to flow out across the dry plains inland for irrigation purposes, instead of simply running into the sea off the east coast which has plenty of rain anyway. On their way through the mountains these massive rivers generate enormous quantities of electricity, a superb piece of engineering. It was all extremely impressive. Australia undoubtedly thinks big, in many different ways, these days.

Then we drove ourselves by car from Sydney to Brisbane, taking eight days to do it, stopping mostly in motels, which are highly developed in Australia and of a good standard. We flew up to Gladstone and went over to Heron Island, on the

Great Barrier Reef for three days. This is a real coral island, with an excellent chalet-type hotel. It is also the nesting place of vast numbers of birds—more than half a million noddy terns in the trees, quarter of a million sooty shearwaters, also known as mutton birds, in the sand and among the tree roots. The latter come in only at night and make the wierdest noises all night long, billing and cooing all over the island. We went looking for them in the darkness with torches, and I took some flash shots of them from only four or five feet away. One guest left his chalet door open and found a pair making love on his bed when he returned.

Huge turtles also crawl up on the beach to lay their eggs, totally unabashed by visitors who stand and watch them. Their little ones hatch out later and are often lured into the bar by the lights. Every now and then, to save them from being trodden on, the guests gather them up in handfuls and throw them into the sea, which is where they were heading anyway.

We flew on, in stages first to Mackay to photograph the sugar industry, then from Townsville to Mount Isa, inland, for the huge copper mine there, and so on to the famous Alice Springs. This is a pretty little town, quite green and lush, surrounded in every direction for hundreds of miles by virtual desert country. We were taken to Ayers Rock, that huge rounded red sandstone hill, standing out over a thousand feet high above the flat desert. At Ross River we tried our hand at throwing boomerangs, so successfully that I had to dodge out of the way when one of mine came whizzing back. Our aboriginal instructor was quite impressed. So was I. He gave me a boomerang and I have tried it out in England. It flatly refuses to behave.

We had a few days in Adelaide, then Melbourne and a short trip to the beautiful island of Tasmania, much less harsh than much of the Outback. Then we flew on from Sydney to Auckland, in New Zealand. This is altogether different country, varying from tropical in the north to great snowy mountains in the south.

We stayed at Rotorua, in the North Island, amidst the geysirs and the pools of boiling mud, where there are many Maoris, and we saw how well they integrate with the white people. Here we fished for trout in lakes and rivers. Fabulous is the only word to describe the trout fishing in New Zealand. We caught so many fish that we had to give most of them away.

We landed on a glacier in a small plane high up on Mount Cook, and we flew through the mountains, not over them, from Queenstown to Milford Sound, just about the most hair-raising flying we have ever done. Yet there has never been an accident on this route, operated by Tourist Air Travel Ltd. The pilot tells his passengers what they are seeing, turns off frequently to see something special and you never know what to expect next. He flew low over a high mountain lake, right to the edge where it plunges over a cliff and we took off, as it were, with the waterfall, known as the Sutherland Falls. Milford Sound is just like a Norwegian fjord, and indeed this whole area is called the Fiordland National Park.

We were most impressed with New Zealand, its beauties, its great mountains and above all its friendly people. Wherever you went people wanted to help us, to take us round and show us the country they are so obviously proud of. A farmer offered to stop work all the following day in one place, to guide us round his district. Alas, if we had only had more time. We did a lot of motoring in New Zealand, quite a bit of flying and even some bus travelling. Uncrowded, beautiful, full of novelties, and with a pleasant climate, it deserves far more visitors.

We flew on to Fiji and here we were right back in the tropics. We explored much of the main island, Viti Levu, including Suva, the capital, and then we went on a three day cruise through the Yasawa Islands. This was sheer romance, cruising about among tropical islands, going into peaceful lagoons, visiting a village where the natives put on a great feast for us under the palm trees on the beach in the moonlight. Then they danced and we listened to their strange and haunting music. In one lagoon our sleek white cruiser, which carried only sixteen passengers, actually tied up to a palm tree and the captain called out that we would stay there for a couple of hours for bathing. Most of us just jumped overboard into the warm blue-green waters. All this was pure heaven.

Flying on to Honolulu, we crossed the International Date Line, so that we arrived in the evening of the day before we left Fiji. Honolulu is a magnificent city, spreading now far back from the famous Waikiki Beach. It is too big and too crowded, certainly, but very beautiful and we liked it. After a few days we flew to the island of Maui where we spent Christmas at a chalet type hotel on Lahaina Beach. Here we relaxed for the holiday period, though each day we added to our photographs. How could we do otherwise in glorious sunshine, with big rollers crashing on the beach and the air warm and pleasant? At Christmas time!

It was autumn weather at San Francisco, with misty mornings followed by gentle sunshine all day long. This is one of the most beautiful big cities anywhere in the world, one we love to roam around. We went out on the vast harbour, across both the great bridges, to Fisherman's Wharf for an unforgettable fish dinner, and one day we were taken out to the Napa Valley to see the famous vineyards. It was most pleasant staying with our friends, the Lloyds, in their lovely private house for a change. They took us to a party given by the Australian Consul nearby. He had just received a copy of the *Daily Telegraph* from home, containing an article of ours on Australia and another one about fishing in New Zealand. Most remarkable timing!

And so to New York, where this early January it was colder than it had been for five years, with a bitter wind, frost and snow. But it still made good pictures, especially the skating in Central Park and views across the East River. London and home, a few days later, seemed quite warm. And that was the end of our Round-the-World trip.

CHAPTER SIXTEEN

India and the Far East Again

In 1968 Paddy Garrow-Fisher asked me if I would like to do another trip for him, this time starting in Delhi and travelling by minibus through Pakistan, Afghanistan and then across northern India. It seemed like a good idea so I said yes, though it would be a pretty rough trip, camping out or using dak bungalows at night, not the height of luxury in India today. Betty was not interested but when our old friend Kushal Singh, the Indian tourist director in London, heard that I was going to India without Betty, he exclaimed:

'This will never do. Betty, I will arrange a trip in India for you while Allan goes off on his minibus.'

And so he did—two weeks all across northern India, from Delhi to Chandigahr, Agra, Jaipur, Udaipur, Lucknow and Patna, with guides and hotels and transport, real V.I.P. treatment. A few years previously we had met the inimitable Boris Lissanevitch, the famous White Russian who had brought tourism to Nepal. He had said that any time we went to Nepal we must stay at his hotel–the Royal, known to every explorer and Everest climber for years—as his guests. Betty wrote to him and was immediately invited to stay at the Royal.

We flew out to Delhi together by Air India, with one stop only, at Moscow. I found my minibus, with only one other passenger as it happened, an elderly American lady, and a very pleasant driver and so, after a couple of days 'doing' Delhi together, Betty and I parted company for six weeks. She was away from home for three weeks altogether and had a marvellous time. More important, she went home with a wonderful collection of pictures, in black and white as well as colour, of many parts of India and the Kathmandu Valley of Nepal. This was a country she fell in love with and she promised to take me there some day! She did, two years later.

My trip took in much new territory and one new country—Afghanistan. We ran into serious riots in Pakistan and had our little bus heavily stoned. Fortunately, no windows were broken and we managed to keep moving, slowly through the angry mobs. Otherwise I might not be writing these words now. We drove up

118

through the Khyber Pass and along some of the splendid new roads in Afghanistan. In Kabul we met one of Paddy's big coaches on its way to India. Down at Mohenjodaro, in southern Pakistan we met another, and spent a night with the passengers. They were a good crowd, mixed in ages all the way from teenagers to elderly people.

Much of our night time accommodation was rough and unnecessarily squalid and I would want to do something better another time. But the whole thing was well worth while. After returning to India we drove for hundreds of miles along the main road between Delhi to Calcutta, the Grand Trunk Road of Rudyard Kipling's *Kim*, and we had to press our way through the same teeming throngs of people, the big herds of cattle and goats and sheep on the road, but now we were menaced by huge over-loaded trucks and buses which rode triumphantly on the crown of the road and refused to budge an inch for anyone. We swallowed more dust than anyone ought to be expected to do in a life time, and our bodies ached with hitting untold numbers of pot holes. But after Benares we turned off on to a quiet and little-used road to Kajuraho, famed for its wonderful old temples with their erotic statuary, and on to Gwalior, a really beautiful old city, swarming with green parakeets. Then finally back to Delhi.

This trip took a whole month, then I had two more weeks myself as the guest of the Indian Tourist Organization. They took me by road to the Sariska Game Reserve and swore that I would see tigers. We drove all among the hills of this beautiful sanctuary, to an ancient temple still in use, hidden among the trees, and we saw lots of game. But no tigers. The chief game warden took a few of us out late at night in a Landrover and we turned off the road and crashed through the bush, across dried-up river beds, all up and down the jungle trails. A warden continually swung a powerful searchlight from side to side, and game of various kinds fled from us in panic. But we saw no tigers. They were not far away, for we found their pug marks, but they were not on show that night.

Then I flew down to Bombay and across the sea north-westwards to Keshod, where I was met by a guide and driven to the guest house in the Gir Forest. Here the tourist people swore I would see lions. Yes, lions in India. This district, now a Game Sanctuary of some five hundred square miles, is the last place in Asia where lions are still found. There are nearly two hundred of them and they are being carefully preserved. At one time lions roamed all the way from Africa to India and beyond, but these are all that are now left of them. The method of seeing these lions was a very different procedure to what I had experienced in Africa. Very different indeed.

Every morning, early, game wardens go out into the forest in pairs, looking for lions lying up after their nightly feeding. The animals sleep most of the day and the wardens know more or less where to look for them. Once a small group has been found, one warden returns to the guest house to report. In the late afternoon he will conduct car loads of visitors—Indians and foreigners—close to the spot where the lions are resting. I had a warden to myself, together with my guide, and a Canadian student by the name of Joslin who was living at the guest house and doing a thesis on the lions. He proved very useful and gave me much information about these unique animals.

We drove some miles into the forest, then got out and actually walked through the trees. Two hundred yards from the road and suddenly, there was a fine male lion in front of me, resting under a tree. He merely raised a sleepy head and dropped it down again. I shot him with my camera. Then the warden pointed out another one, much nearer. I shot him, too. He was just twenty three feet from me, according to my range-finder. Other people came along, with wardens, and the lions showed no more than a passing interest in us. It was uncanny, after Africa, where no one is allowed to get out of a car in lion country. Yet it was apparently quite safe. No lion in the Gir Forest ever attacks human beings, not even the local farmers. They get to know the wardens, apparently, and trust them, though they are completely wild animals. The wardens usually have a small goat with them, tied to a short lead, and this keeps the lions interested and prevents them from wandering away.

The next afternoon we went out earlier, to where a group of three lionesses were lying up. Again, we walked through the forest until we were quite close to them. They began to wake up and started to creep forward, stalking the little goat. When one got too close, perhaps ten feet away, the warden would suddenly stand up and rush forward, so astonishing the lions that I saw one actually fall over backwards, off balance.

Visitors came and went until it was deep dusk, but we were told to stay on. It grew quite dark and the wardens used electric torches to keep an eye on the three lionesses, which were now prowling about very actively. One of the animals took an interest in a tripod holding a small telescope that had been used by the Canadian student while it was still light. I called out to him and he rushed forward just in time to chase the lion away. I was using flash by now and got a shot of this dramatic action. I took various other shots in the dark as we watched the animals. One wandered right round us and Joslin agreed with me that, as it passed, it was not more than seven feet away.

Then the wardens led us some little distance away to where another warden was sitting beside a buffalo calf. The lions followed us closely, very closely, getting ever more excited. The little buffalo was untied, dragged further into the jungle and tied to another tree.

'Now get ready,' I was told, 'this happens very quickly.'

The wardens suddenly rushed back from the buffalo calf and instantly all three lionesses pounced. The poor animal did not live for one second. I was able to get just one flash shot as it was dragged to the ground. Today I believe these killings are shown to the visitors who come late in the afternoon. It is a strange experience.

I flew back to Bombay and then on to Aurangabad, from where I was taken to the famous caves and temples at Ajanta and Ellora. Betty and I had missed them on our previous visit. They are indeed impressive, with their beautiful wall paintings and intricate carvings. And after this it was time for me to go home.

Early one morning I flew from Aurangabad to Bombay, spent the whole day there getting extra pictures, then flew to Delhi on an evening plane, and was taken out to dinner and a night club. I caught the Air India night plane to London and was home the next morning.

Betty told me so much about Nepal, and I was so intrigued with her pictures, that we began to plan a return there. Two years later we made it, spending Christmas in Katmandu and New Year at Pokhara. But first we had a few days in Delhi, and after Nepal we spent a week in Assam. Then we flew on to Singapore and finished up with a fortnight in Ceylon.

I fell for Nepal just as much as Betty had done. We saw much more of it than she had been able to do and we felt sorry for the high-speed tourists who spend only two or three days there. The Katmandu Valley alone takes a week to explore, it is so full of interest and beauty, with its gorgeous temples, its beautiful hills and the vast views of the Himalayan Range gleaming white in the far distance. Each morning started misty but the sun soon came out and then it would be quite warm, even in December, returning quickly to mist and even frost after dark.

We spent a couple of days at the famous Tiger Tops, a hotel in the trees similar to Treetops in Kenya. Here we went out on elephants—the only means of transport from the Megauly air strip—looking for tigers and other game. Our elephant almost trod on a tiger and shied away from it, but all we saw was the tall grass moving violently. But we saw rhinos and various other animals, though not in anything like the numbers we had seen in Africa.

Pokhara is a small town on the shores of Lake Phewa Tal, in an exquisitely beautiful valley, almost over-shadowed by the gleaming icy peaks of Annapurna. We walked along the shore line and we rode in a dug-out canoe on the placid water. One day we walked for miles along the rough trail in the Seti Valley that leads to the high mountains, the trail used by many a famous climber. But we went only as far as a Tibetan refugee village, where I photographed the priest in his gaudy little temple, and we gazed in awe at the great mass of Machhapuchare across the valley. Nepal is really something different; we would gladly have spent many weeks there.

In Assam we motored up to Shillong, a famous old hill station, and then went down into the broad valley of the Brahmaputra, through the tea gardens and on to the Kaziranga Game Sanctuary. The great attraction here is the Indian rhino, and we went looking for them on the back of an elephant. They are found in swampy ground, amidst bushes and dense tall grasses, along with deer and various other animals. We found the rhinos everywhere and they generally looked at us resentfully and moved slowly away. But round one corner we suddenly came upon one with a youngster, and she did not like us at all. She charged straight at us and our elephant began to scream and get very restive. The mother rhino was only stopped in her tracks by the warden firing a couple of shots in front of her nose. Had the elephant panicked and run, we would doubtless have been thrown off her back, a daunting thought. I found that I had continued taking photographs even during these tense moments, and got one shot of the animals at full speed.

Singapore was a great surprise. It had grown enormously since our last visit, but more important, its growth had been carefully planned and executed, so that today it is, without a doubt, one of the most beautiful cities in the world. Much of this goes to the credit of the Prime Minister, Lee Kuan Yew, who at the time of independence in 1959, was regarded by many as a dangerous communist. Now he is universally recognized as one of the world's great statesmen.

We used Qantas planes everywhere on this long trip between countries, the next stage being to Ceylon. Here we did a lot of work for the Ceylon Tourist Organization, who treated us very well indeed. We had an excellent guide and car and we travelled over many parts of the country, north to the ancient cities of Polonnaruwa and Anuradhapura, up into the mountains to Kandy and Nuwara Eliya, then down to the southern coast. We saw wild elephants and much other game in the Yalla National Park, then drove all round the south-west coast, through the old Portuguese town of Galle and past busy little fishing ports to Mount Lavinia. Here our hosts had thoughtfully planned a whole free day for us, bathing and relaxing after our quite strenuous two weeks in their beautiful country.

CHAPTER SEVENTEEN

Both Sides of the Red Sea

I made two journeys by myself, in 1969 and 1970, which proved highly successful, the first to Saudi Arabia and the second to Ethiopia. Saudi Arabia is not a tourist country, but I concentrated on the modernization of this strange and bleak desert kingdom. I was there in winter time; in the summer heat it must be intolerable. I found it fascinating, but I had trouble persuading some of my guides to work in the afternoons. They had to have lunch then a sleep and finally prayers. By which time there was little daylight left. But somehow I managed.

I started at Jeddah, drove inland to Taef on a stupendous mountain road, bypassing Mecca where, as a non-Moslem, I would have been far from welcome, then flew to Riyadh, the capital, and on to Dhahran, on the Persian Gulf—sorry, the Arabian Gulf, if you live on the west side of it. I photographed the oil port of Ras Tanura and the huge refinery close by, and I drove far out into the desert to see some of the oil wells and the vast fire pits where the surplus gas is burnt off, a weird sight. From Riyadh and from Dhahran I was taken to some of the huge oases in the desert, where at al Ahssa in particular, vast irrigation projects were under way. Tens of thousands of acres of the desert are being restored to cultivation, hundreds of miles of canals are being built, vast quantities of good soil are being laid on the desert sands and whole areas are protected by tree belts so that the drifting sands will not take over again. It was all most impressive and made good pictures. The enormous oil revenues are now being used wisely and well, not only in this respect but in building colleges and universities, a vast network of first class roads all over the country, improved housing and in countless other ways. I would gladly go back to Saudi Arabia again any time to see how these projects are progressing.

I went to Ethiopia because a good friend of mine, John Blower, was then the chief game warden, and he aroused my interest. How different this remote country is from Saudi Arabia. Surrounded on all sides virtually by the greatest deserts in the world, it is a surprisingly green and pleasant country. It really consists of a vast block of mountains, with the main plateau standing six to eight thousand feet above sea level, and ranges of mountains higher still. Hence it catches much rain and is well watered. Right through the centre runs the Rift Valley which starts in the Jordan Valley and goes on into Central Africa. Here, as in Kenya, there is a string of lakes down in the valley, each one a natural bird sanctuary.

Addis Ababa, the capital, is a strange mixture of old and very new modern buildings, with lots of space between them, where cows and sheep graze undisturbed in fields right alongside business premises. I went far and wide all over the country, sometimes by air, to places like Dire Dawa, Jimma and Asmara, at other times by Landrover, with a good guide-driver. We went off for a week to the Rift Valley and the Awash National Park.

I was fascinated with the bird life everywhere; it was obvious as soon as I arrived in the country. Ethiopia is by no means over-populated. There are great expanses of virtually empty countryside and mountains where birds thrive unmolested. Insecticides and the like have had little if any effect so far on wild life, and there seems to be little hunting. No one so far has made a proper study of the birds of Ethiopia. There are known to be at least twenty-six species that are found nowhere else, and it is a great country for migratory birds from Africa to Europe and Asia. What a chance for some enterprising ornithologist.

The scenery of Ethiopia is magnificent, a great mixture of gentle country scenes, with graceful groups of trees and clusters of 'tukuls', native houses, and breath-taking panoramas of great valleys with vast blue mountains in the distance. There are gorges, such as that of the Blue Nile, which almost rival the Grand Canyon, and endless tumbling ranges of wild and rocky mountains, best seen from the air. I spent a night at Harar, and went out after dark to watch an old man feeding wild hyaenas by hand, a highly risky business indeed. I took many flash pictures, with the revolting creatures running all round me, quite unperturbed.

I spent my last week in Ethiopia doing the Historic Route. This is a five day air trip organized by Ethiopian Airlines between Addis Ababa and Asmara, operating both ways, with five overnight stops at quite good hotels. I flew on an early morning plane from Addis to Bahar Dar, on the southern shore of Lake Tana, the source of the Blue Nile. Sight-seeing trips are laid on at each stopping place. Here it was to the Tissisat Falls, a spectacular waterfall on the Blue Nile twenty miles downstream. At Gondar, city of the old Ethiopian Kings, sixty miles north across the Lake, there are more than twenty castles, in quite a modern little town, beautifully situated among lofty green hills.

Next came Lalibela, a strange and remote small town nine thousand feet above sea level. Here, many centuries ago, King Lalibela sought refuge as a Christian—most of the Ethiopians are Christians—from Moslem persecutors. This spot is so remote that he thought it a safe place in which to build his New Jerusalem. Many churches were carved out of the living rock and they survive to this day, most of them still in use. No road leads to Lalibela, the only means of access being by air or long trails through the mountains on horseback.

Then comes Axum, believed to be the home of the Queen of Sheba. The ruins of her palace and bathing pool are still there, but the pool is now reduced to a patch of mud round a spring where donkeys are loaded with goat skins full of water. At

Axum there are a number of stele, tall pillars of granite, some of them carrying elaborate carving. Their origin is somewhat mysterious and they may be two thousand years old. Priests in the old church brought out priceless, gem encrusted crowns and crosses for me to photograph in the sunlight.

Asmara, the end of the route going north, is a modern city built largely by the Italians when they occupied Ethiopia before the war. The citizens of Asmara consider Addis Ababa to be a primitive and dirty place, and rather scorn it. I don't agree. The capital is by far the more attractive city in every way, though less modern in some respects.

I spent one day going down the escarpment from Asmara on a magnificent Italian-built road to Massawa, on the Red Sea. Dropping down from the cool heights of the plateau, we were soon in suffocating heat, a different climate altogether. I photographed the town and the docks of Massawa, had lunch at the Red Sea Hotel, and then we drove back up the long winding hill to the cool heights again, a great relief. I flew home in an Ethiopian Boeing 707, carrying a total of twenty passengers.

CHAPTER EIGHTEEN

Conclusion

So this how we try to cover the world with our cameras and pens, with half a dozen trips abroad each year, and two or three in our own islands. Suggestions for new journeys, to new countries, often come quite unexpectedly, from a variety of sources.

There is so much more I could tell you about other parts of the world that we have seen, but there is not much room left in this book. I must mention one or two more trips before I finish, though.

Years ago, after our first Far Eastern trip, the editor of one of the glossy magazines, wagging an admonishing finger at us, said:

'It is all very well to have pictures of Hong Kong, Japan and India in your library, but do you realize that you have nothing of Greece, Yugoslavia, many parts of Italy, Austria and Scandinavia? Why don't you do something about it?'

We did, the next year. We set off in our car early in March, crossed France to the Riviera, motored slowly all the way down Italy to the extreme south, took our car across to Corfu by ship, then spent a month touring all over Greece. From Thessalonika we drove northwards into Yugoslavia, over the Montenegrin Mountains to the Dalmatian Coast, up to Venice and the Dolomites, then all through Austria, across Germany and by sea to Sweden. Here we covered most of the south and drove into Norway, leisurely across to Bergen where we parked our car and did the coastal cruise to the North Cape and back. We were away for four and a half months, working all the time. Yet each frontier we crossed seemed to recharge our batteries as it were, and we never found we were too tired. And so we added thousands of new pictures to our library and several new countries. It was strenuous but it was worth it. Altogether, we covered over 10,000 miles.

I have only mentioned East Africa and its fabulous wild animals in passing. We have done more than one trip there, apart from the first occasion, on our around-Africa cruise. We explored much of Kenya in the autumn of 1962, then sailed down the coast of East Africa from Mombasa to Beira, in Moçambique, on the British India ship UGANDA. Here the Portuguese showed us over much of their big colony for ten days or so, and we caught the same ship back again to Dar es Salaam, spending Christmas on board. We flew to Zanzibar and after that we motored far up into the interior of Tanzania, to Arusha and Lake Manyara, deep in the Great Rift Valley.

The Lake Manyara National Park is one of the smallest, but contains more animals per square mile than any other we have ever seen. It is here that, for reasons quite unknown, lions climb trees, and we took pictures of them resting in the branches. We also went to the Ngorongoro Crater, a vast extinct volcano that is a natural game sanctuary in itself, teeming with countless wild animals. We flew home on this occasion to a bitter cold January, still in our tropical clothes.

In 1965 and 1966 we were invited by British India to go on school cruises, first on the DEVONIA to Greece and Crete, the second to the Baltic, on the NEVASA. These ships carry hundreds of school children but also a number of ordinary passengers. It is an educational cruise for the children, and very much so for the passengers as well, if they want it. They can attend the lectures and film shows about the places to be visited and everyone goes ashore together, with excellent local guides and transport. We have just done another of these cruises, this time to Iceland and Norway, on the UGANDA, now converted. To us, these are far more interesting than normal cruises with their crowds and, so often, too much organized activity.

In 1957 Kodak's organized big exhibitions of the work of seven different photographers in their Kingsway building. I was one of the favoured seven, the others being Eric Hosking, Tony Armstrong-Jones, as he then was, Cornell Lucas, Joe Waldorf, Percy Hennell and Mike Davis. The theme of my exhibition was to be 'Travel with your Camera', and it was to cover all the countries I had so far visited. Many shipping and air lines were to be represented, as well as the countries concerned. But I had not so far flown with B.O.A.C., so they took me down to Nigeria and Ghana, where I spent seven weeks covering both countries pretty thoroughly.

In Ghana I did a complete photographic coverage of all the activities of the Gliksten timber company, from searching in the jungle for good trees to cutting them down, hauling the logs out to the nearest road and either to a saw mill or to the harbour at Takoradi for shipment abroad. It was hot and exhausting but I added two more countries to my library and a mass of photographs of far more than merely tourist interest. It was one of the most successful trips I have ever done. And I got pictures of B.O.A.C. planes at Kano and Lagos, for the exhibition.

Mrs Pandit, the Indian High Commissioner at that time, graciously consented to open my exhibition. We had nearly four hundred guests at the opening. K.L.M. flew over bouquets of flowers that morning from Holland for Mrs. Pandit and Betty, and four hundred rose button-holes for all the guests. Switzerland, Norway and Holland kindly sent girls in native costumes, B.O.A.C., B.E.A., Cunard and others sent stewardesses or hostesses, all in uniform, so that, with Indian ladies in saris, and a Sikh in a turban, Kodak's, Kingsway, looked a pretty gay place that opening night.

A count of visitors was kept for each exhibition and mine topped twenty thousand in the month it was open. We secured forty full pages of publicity in a wide variety of magazines, and numerous articles in the press as well. All this certainly did me no harm; it was the most valuable publicity imaginable. I have always been grateful to Kodaks, not only for this exhibition, but for the many different ways in which they have helped me over many years, and for the most friendly relationship we have enjoyed at all times. I hope I have given them something in return.

Perhaps I have tended to emphasize the more distant countries I have covered; the glamour of foreign places always seems to go up in direct proportion to the distance one travels. I hope I have not neglected Europe and Mediterranean countries too much. We have been, at one time or another, to every country in Europe, some several times, and to most of the big islands, such as Malta, Sicily, Sardinia, Rhodes, Corsica, Crete, Cyprus and Majorca. Each is really worthy of a chapter on its own. And all the North African countries, Morocco, Tunisia, Egypt, besides Israel, Jordan and Lebanon. I could say so much about them all, or so much more than I have been able to do.

We have not finished travelling yet, not by a long way. We have recently merged our business with a larger company, as you will see in the final chapter, but we still go on, travelling and photographing. Even while I have been writing this book, more trips have loomed up and indeed, this is a new final paragraph to this particular chapter, because we have just been out to the Far East again, to Japan, Hong Kong, Macau and Thailand, after I thought I had finished writing this book! We are getting rather tired of long air trips nowadays, and much prefer travelling by sea, as in the past. So we have started to organise some sea travel and already have five cruises lined up between now and June, 1974. It will be nice to travel more leisurely for a change, and of course pictures taken on board ship are as valuable as any taken anywhere.

The Business Side

I have said a lot about travelling and taking photographs but now, what happens to the films once they have been exposed? All our colour films are processed outside the office, in recent years by Morgan and Swan, Ltd., in London. They give us an excellent service and their processing has been consistently good.

I develop my black-and-white films myself. Years ago I had them done out, but the company concerned gave up doing monochrome and I have never found anyone to replace them. I develop eighteen rolls of 120 film at a time, on spools in a three gallon tank, using Microdol-X film. By topping up with replenisher each time, I find I can develop a hundred and fifty films quite safely with each three gallons of developer.

It takes me some twenty minutes to load the spools, another ten to fifteen minutes to develop them, ten minutes for fixing and half an hour for washing, in running water. I sponge down each film before drying, and this takes about another twenty minutes. I can do something else while the films are washing, but the total time for developing a batch of eighteen films is well under two hours. And I get exactly the sort of negatives I want.

Contact prints are made immediately in our darkrooms, two sets from each film, on glossy glazed paper, with the number of the film stamped on the back of each print. The prints are cut up, leaving a narrow black border all round. One set remains with the films, the other set is put into small envelopes, one film to an envelope, with the number on the outside, and they are given to me.

I sort out the contact prints into subjects, dividing and subdividing so that, for convenience, I finish up with not more than a dozen prints on each one. These go into separate small envelopes, with the subjects written on the outside. I then put all these envelopes in order, perhaps in the order in which the subjects were taken, or any other arrangement that seems to make sense, and number them. The same subject sometimes appears on more than one film. All the contacts go into the same envelope, being split up if there are too many. The corresponding negatives are easily found later by referring to the film numbers on the backs of the prints.

When I am taking photographs, I always number my films and make notes to help me identify the pictures later. I still have all my note books, even from pre-war years, and very valuable they often are. I find that it is not sufficient, though, merely to make a note of the name of a place. So many of the pictures tend to look alike later on. I frequently add bits of description such as 'sun on right, or left; church with spire; white building on hill; small ship approaching;' and so on. If a clock appears in the picture I always note the time—most useful later. However many notes one makes, they are never enough, especially when someone slips up on the number of a film.

Having numbered my envelopes, I then go through each one, marking the unwanted prints with a cross in ink across their faces. The rest are put in order for numbering. I find that only a small percentage are rejected. A few may be underexposed, people may be awkwardly placed, or they may have moved too rapidly, I may have shaken the camera (oh, yes, we all do it at times) or I may just dislike a picture for some reason. I am quite ruthless; I just sling them all out.

I mark up a cross-section of the retained ones for printing, using metal masks in three sizes that give me the proportion of a 10 × 8 inch print. My printer then numbers all the selected prints in order, finds the negatives and puts the prints in with them, each in a separate small envelope, with the negative number written on the outside. The marked-up negatives are put aside for printing, and follow the rest in due course to be filed in steel cabinets, each capable of holding about 1,500 negatives, quite a capital investment.

The second set of contact prints is numbered in the same way, the rejects with their negatives being discarded. The numbered ones are then pasted into large albums, in numerical order, with short captions, and the name of the country on the outside. We have nearly three hundred books. Negative numbers of each country are prefixed with two letters, such as CD for Canada, TK for Turkey, AR for Argentine, and so on. These albums are made specially for us and are guaranteed never to fall to pieces, no matter how much they are used. So far none has collapsed, and they are used extensively, year in and year out. We use them ourselves all the time, for making selections of prints, and they are used by many of our clients when they come up to the office for pictures. They are our bible; we could not do without them.

Our monochrome contacts are made by laying the negatives in strips of four on a sheet of 10 × 8 inch glossy paper, pressing them down with a piece of plate glass, and exposing under an enlarger. One film cut into three such strips, just fills one sheet of paper. We make contacts from our colour films in exactly the same way, but twice over, as it were. The first time, of course, we produce negatives. After drying and glazing, this negative sheet is laid face down on to another piece of the same paper and we print through it. Despite the paper, the quality is surprisingly good. We use our albums of colour contacts similarly for selection purposes, as it saves time and avoids handling the colour itself too much. We do not need to put a contact print in with the transparency because we never make colour prints. We employ the same prefix for numbering our colour pictures but add C as well, to denote colour. CDC for Canada, TKC for Turkey, and so on. Then, when picture numbers are used, we always know whether they refer to monochrome or colour.

Prints from our marked up negatives are made at once, two of each, and put into stock. Our chief librarian sees them before they are put away, so that she knows what new material we have produced. I myself often take out a few of these first prints to illustrate articles we plan to write, but there is always at least one put into stock. Any other prints, from the unmarked negatives, which may be selected in the future, are printed as required, again two of each, one going into stock. We keep all our 10 × 8 inch stock prints in the boxes from which the paper originally came, a most convenient arrangement.

Colour transparencies are kept in individual see-through envelopes, with a small label stuck on the outside giving the number and a brief caption. We have the labels specially printed, with our name and address on them. Ten of these envelopes are placed in open-ended manilla envelopes, marked with the numbers on the outside (e.g. CDC–81 to 90) and these are kept in small cardboard boxes on shelves.

We operate a card index system of all our pictures, colour and monochrome, and are continually adding to it. Everything we can think of goes on to cards, not only name places but headings such as rivers, rough seas, pets, birds, bridges, cows, trees, children, etc. One can never over-do a card index. Ours is never complete enough but it is extremely useful.

We send a delivery note out with every batch of pictures that leaves our office. On the ones for colour there is printed a warning about losing or damaging these originals. We claim up to £100 for a lost or damaged transparency and have often got it. Monochrome prints not returned are no great loss, but colour is. One job in the office that has to be done constantly is to go through the loose-leaf books in which our copies of delivery notes are kept, to check up on pictures which are outstanding, especially colour. It is surprising, sometimes dismaying, to discover how much material has not been returned, and also at times how much has been published and about which we have not been informed. I don't mean that our clients are deliberately dishonest, but in some cases, somewhere along the line, someone has slipped up and even editors do not know that their routine has not been followed to the end.

Our pictures are used in a wide variety of ways, less in the way of feature stories now but much more for illustrative purposes, in articles, books, encyclopaedias, advertisements, travel brochures, television as still shots, calendars and so on. I am constantly surprised at the wide use to which they are put, and the often unexpected requests we receive. It seems that we could photograph anything on earth and sooner or later someone would want it.

Building up this big library has, of course, meant taking on additional staff from time to time. At first we took on Mack, our quite invaluable printer. Next, I had to have a secretary to assist with all the clerical work. Then I reached the stage where I had to have an office manager, someone who knew this peculiar business thoroughly and could sell pictures, deal with clients, send out selections on approval, contact people and supervise all the work of the staff. This was a big move and quite a gamble.

I found a man—Eric Pothecary—who had been with various Fleet Street picture agencies all his life but wanted a change. He stayed with us for seven years and helped me considerably to build up the business. Most important, perhaps, I could go away for any length of time and know that someone competent was looking after the office and could cope with whatever happened. Because he was there, for instance, we could contemplate our nine months' trip to the Far East, and our four months' trip through Europe. Without an office manager we would have been pinned to the office more and more, an impossible situation.

We have had an office manager ever since. Pothecary left after some seven years for a top job with P.A.-Reuters, at a salary I could not match. Others came and went after various periods and now we have a charming Irishman, in the name of Ronald Kearney. He knew little of our kind of business but was an experienced administrator. He soon picked up the essentials and his office experience made him an excellent manager.

Our chief librarian—Jean Clark—is well known now in the business. She was introduced by Eric Pothecary and soon got on to the job. She is extraordinarily conscientious and has done a splendid job over many years. She has had to train new girls who came in as library assistants from time to time, as well as look after the constantly increasing demands for our pictures, no easy task.

Kim Read, another girl who came to us many years ago, left after a few years to work at the B.B.C., nearer to her home. But one day, after a year or so, she phoned me up and asked if she could come back. We needed more help just then and she knew our business, so we were glad to welcome her once more. She is now assistant librarian and a splendid worker.

Now, all this has taken many years to achieve. We have built up a library that seems to be well known, and we have done an ever-increasing business with a steadily expanding clientele. We have amassed somewhere near half a million pictures in the library but are far too busy to make an accurate count. But time goes on and we do not get any younger.

In recent years we began to wonder how we could eventually retire, or at least gradually take things easier and shed some of our responsibilities. A partner would have been a possibility, as we had no son to take over the business, but no one turned up who seemed suitable. So I began to let it be known that I was open to some sort of offer, to negotiate some suitable arrangement.

A few firms were interested. A big publishing firm—one of our clients—declared that it would be useful to have our library in their organization, but whereas we were running it profitably, they would have it in the red in no time. An American publisher was looking for libraries to buy, but seemed to us to be only interested in transferring everything abroad. This I would not have agreed to anyway, as I had some conscience about my staff, and would not have liked to see my business just die and disappear, whatever I was offered for it. Then something much more promising turned up.

For many years we had done a two-way business with Replicards Limited, one of London's leading photographic trade printing houses which is backed by a complete Exhibition and Display Contracting Service. One of Replicards specialities is a unique Photomural service and on many occasions they had used my library prints in this field. We in turn had used their services for Photoprinting and mounting work too large for our own darkroom to cope with. In 1971 we began talking about the possibility of a merger. Replicards were expanding and wanted to acquire a photo-library which they could develop into one of the most comprehensive in the country. Ours seemed to be the foundation they were looking for and a satisfactory business arrangement was concluded.

Replicards were most anxious that I should continue to be closely associated with the library, that I should go on taking photographs, travelling and writing articles as before. The name would remain the same, the staff and the premises unchanged, only now it would be a limited company. In fact, our clients would not notice any difference.

I received a lump sum to invest for our old age when it comes. I was kept on on a retainer, to continue travelling and photographing as before, but I was no longer responsible for running the business.

Neither Betty nor I want to retire yet. We both still have the wanderlust and want to go on exploring the world. But we were getting rather tired of all the responsibility of running our own business. It was a relief to shed all this and let someone else deal with it. We could enjoy our travelling more now.

We signed our merger agreement on July 1st, 1972 and the next day Betty and I went off to Holland for three days, then up the Rhine from Rotterdam to Basle on the latest of the luxury K-D Line ships, and finished up with two weeks in Arosa, in Switzerland. Many years before, we had published a long article on our favourite winter sports resort in the Tatler, with colour and monochrome pictures. We called it simply: 'We Like Arosa'. The Arosa tourist people were delighted and sent us a cable ending up with: 'We like the Cashes'.

They invited us to stay at Arosa any time we liked for two weeks as their guests. For years we had thought about it but other things seemed to be more pressing. At last we were doing it. And very nicely the Arosa people looked after us, putting us up in the Park Hotel in great luxury. Unfortunately our old friend Werner Grob the tourist director, who had just retired and was going to take us around, was seriously ill. We saw him in hospital and cheered him up quite a lot. But he died soon after we returned home, a sad end to a very warm friendship.

We seem to be as busy as ever, despite the merger, but we enjoy it all now in a new way. Within the first year of our agreement we have been abroad six times, to Holland, Germany and Switzerland, to the Ionian Islands, to Madeira, to Crete, to Italy, and to Corsica and the Riviera. We have also done four trips in Britain, to Yorkshire, Pembrokeshire, the Lake District and the Welsh Valleys. Now, as I write these final words, we are on a school cruise on the British India ship UGANDA, to Iceland and Norway, and we have those five new cruises to look forward to in the near future.

I am free to do any writing I like (hence this book, among other things), and I can take on commissions. These are often excellent means of getting pictures for the library in addition to the commissioned work. And so the pattern of our later years is taking shape, Some day, perhaps, we shall reach the stage where we no longer wish to go travelling, when possibly we won't even want to take photographs, though I simply cannot imagine it. Nor can I imagine ever wanting to stop writing. Who knows, I might even try fiction in my old age! Meanwhile I continue to expend a lot of physical energy on our garden, which is a splendid change from poring over pictures and pounding a typewriter.

Replicards have already negotiated to represent other leading photographers and to absorb their work into the library on an agency basis; their original idea is taking shape very satisfactorily. The superb work of Eileen Ramsey, the first photographer whose work has been incorporated into the library, is widely known and admired. She has specialized for many years in yachting and sailing, a subject that nicely augments our own photographs. Other arrangements are in the offing and I can see the whole thing becoming a big success.

Finally, for anyone wishing to become a successful freelance photo-journalist, I think the essential ingredients are, first, to be able to take good photographs of high quality and to maintain and improve the quality at all times; second, to be reasonably business-like and to run the business efficiently; third, to be quick to seize opportunities and to make the most of them; fourth, to be able to talk to prospective clients in a convincing way, to establish their confidence in you; fifth, to be truly dedicated to one's work and prepared to work all hours, day or night, in the interests of the job; sixth, to always employ a good accountant to keep your financial affairs in order; and finally, to have faith in yourself; never doubt that you will succeed.

Technical Details

I have purposely not mentioned the cameras we use, because I am a great believer in every photographer using the sort of camera that suits him best. We find that the best camera for all our general work is the Rolleiflex. It just happens to suit us both and we feel happier with it than with any other make or type. I also use a Pentax, with a variety of lenses, for special work, such as animal photography or where 35 mm. negatives or transparencies are required. I like this camera very much indeed.

For many years we have used only Kodak films, Verichrome Pan 120 and Ektachrome X 120 for normal work, but Tri-X and EH where more speed is required. With my Pentax I use Plus X, Tri-X, Ektachrome X or H, as required. I often rate EH film at 800 ASA and have the processing modified accordingly.

We are strong believers in not carrying too much equipment around with us. One can waste a lot of time changing cameras and lenses instead of just getting on with the job with one or two cameras that will do nearly everything possible.